SECOND EDITION

MUSIC THEORY for Young Musicians

grade 2

Study Notes with Exercises for ABRSM

Name : ....

Address : ....

Phone : ....

YING YING NG

Published by:

poco STUDIO

Poco Studio Sdn Bhd (646228-V)
B-2-8, IOI Boulevard, Jalan Kenari 5, Bandar Puchong Jaya, 47170 Puchong, Selangor, Malaysia
Tel/Fax: +603 8074 0086   poco_studio@yahoo.co.uk   www.pocostudio.org   facebook.com/pocostudio

Copyright © 2006, 2012 by Poco Studio Sdn Bhd

All rights reserved. No part of this document may be reproduced or transmitted in any form or by any means, electronic, mechanical, photocopying, recording, or otherwise, without prior written permission of Poco Studio Sdn Bhd.

Copyediting by David C. L. Ngo BAI, PhD, SMIEEE

Printed in Malaysia

ISBN: 978-967-10003-2-8

PREFACE

Designed as a workbook to suit the needs of today's young pupils and their teachers, this series presents music theory in a very easy to understand and practical format. Here are some of the pedagogical principles adopted, which make this series unique:

Problem Solving: Breaking a problem into smaller parts makes solving it easier. This series isolates a problem, breaks it into small, manageable parts, and then merges it back into the bigger picture.

Repetition: The key to learning music theory is repetition. Under the lesson plan, the pupil studies component parts incrementally, applying previously acquired skills in the repetitive drills of subsequent lessons.

Association: Children will not learn if repetition is dull. The series creates a fantasy world by using pictures, cartoons and stories to introduce new key words and concepts; this arouses the interest and invokes the imagination of the child, thereby aiding retention of the information.

Challenge: Examinations can provide a challenge to the pupil. This series covers the latest revisions outlined by the Associated Board of the Royal Schools of Music for their theory examinations. It uses effective and efficient drills and exercises that progressively teach the basic concepts. The material is simplified to suit the child's level. The examples and exercises build on language and concepts that children already have, culminating in the acquisition of the skills and knowledge vital to passing the examination.

NOTES ON THE SECOND EDITION
The second edition of Music Theory for Young Musicians brings the practice exercises and examples in the text up to date with the latest ABRSM exam requirements. It also includes many clarifications that update the presentation of the ideas and concepts in the book and thus improve its logical flow. It adds a specimen test in the exam format and provides a set of revision notes on the key areas. All exercises and examples have been revised and many new exercise drills have been added. Concept explanations have been simplified to make it easier to understand. The book's layout has been made clearer by putting the main text against a white background. Additionally, a background colour has been given to each information note to make it more visually inviting.

ACKNOWLEDGE
Cover design and assistance with the illustrations by Amos Tai is gratefully acknowledged. I also extend my sincere thanks to the following persons for advice and suggestions as reviewers of the draft:

- Margaret O'Sullivan Farrell BMus, DipMus, LTCL
  Course Director, Lecturer in Keyboard Studies
  DIT Conservatory of Music and Drama, Dublin, Ireland

- Dr. Ita Beausang BMus, MA, PhD, LRAM
  Former Acting Director, Lecturer in Musicianship Studies
  DIT Conservatory of Music and Drama, Dublin, Ireland

Their suggestions for its improvement have helped immeasurably to make it a useful and practical workbook. My grateful thanks also go to my family, David, Alethia and Natasha, for their patience and love that have allowed me to pursue this project.

Ying Ying Ng

CONTENTS

- 4   Ledger Lines
- 9   Time Names and Time Values
- 11   Time Signatures
- 16   Triplets
- 19   Grouping of Notes
- 23   Grouping of Rests
- 28   The Scales and Key Signatures of A, B♭ and E♭ Major
- 37   The Scales and Key Signatures of A, E and D Minor
- 43   Tonic Triads
- 46   Degrees of the Scale
- 48   Intervals
- 50   Composing Four-Bar Rhythms
- 53   Performance Directions
- 56   General Exercises
- 59   Specimen Test Grade 2
- 62   Revision Notes

Ledger Lines

A **ledger line** is a short line added above/below a staff to extend its range.

Notes on ledger lines in treble clef

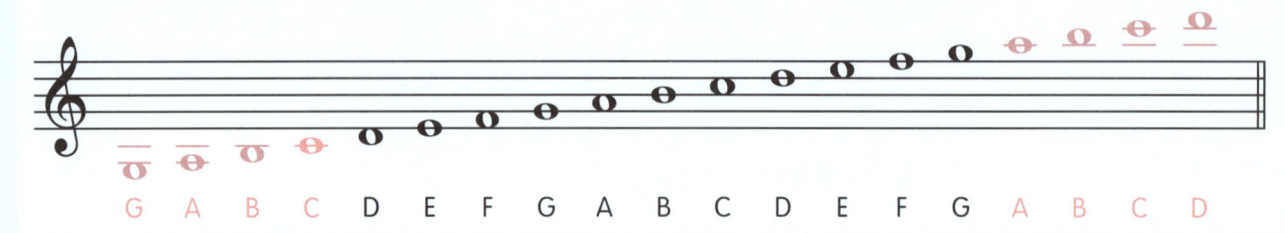

G A B C D E F G A B C D E F G A B C D

1 Trace and copy the notes and their letter names.

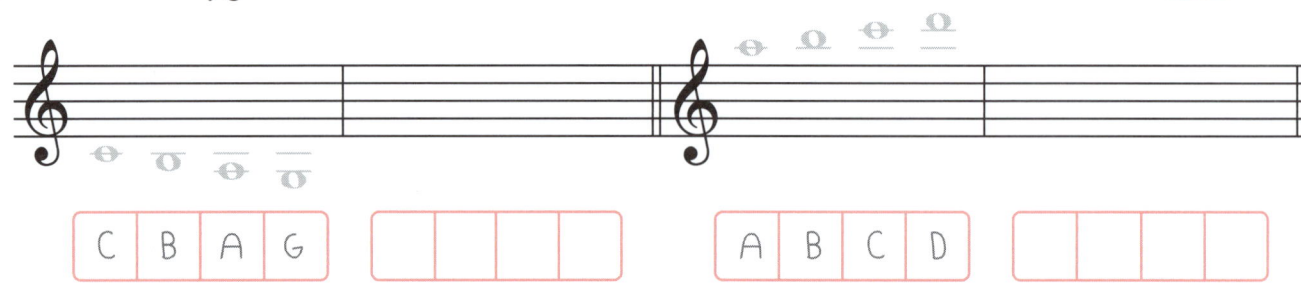

C B A G ☐ ☐ ☐   A B C D ☐ ☐ ☐

2 Fill in the missing notes as semibreves (whole notes) and their letter names.

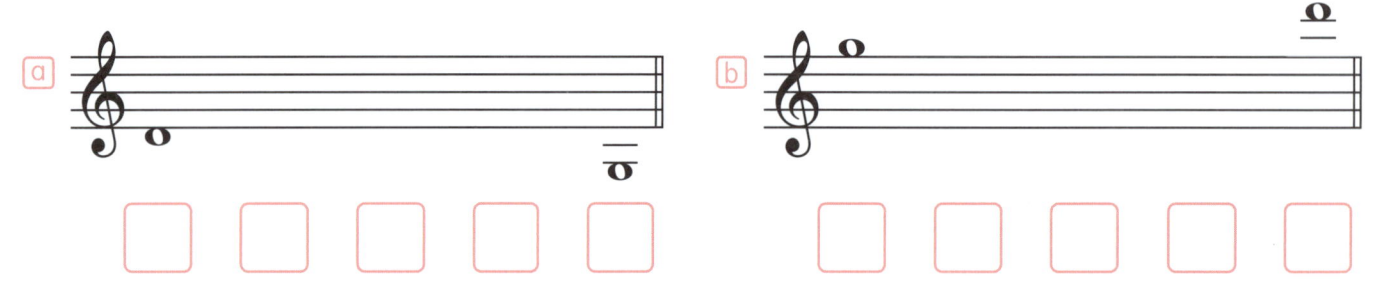

a

b

3 Write the letter names.

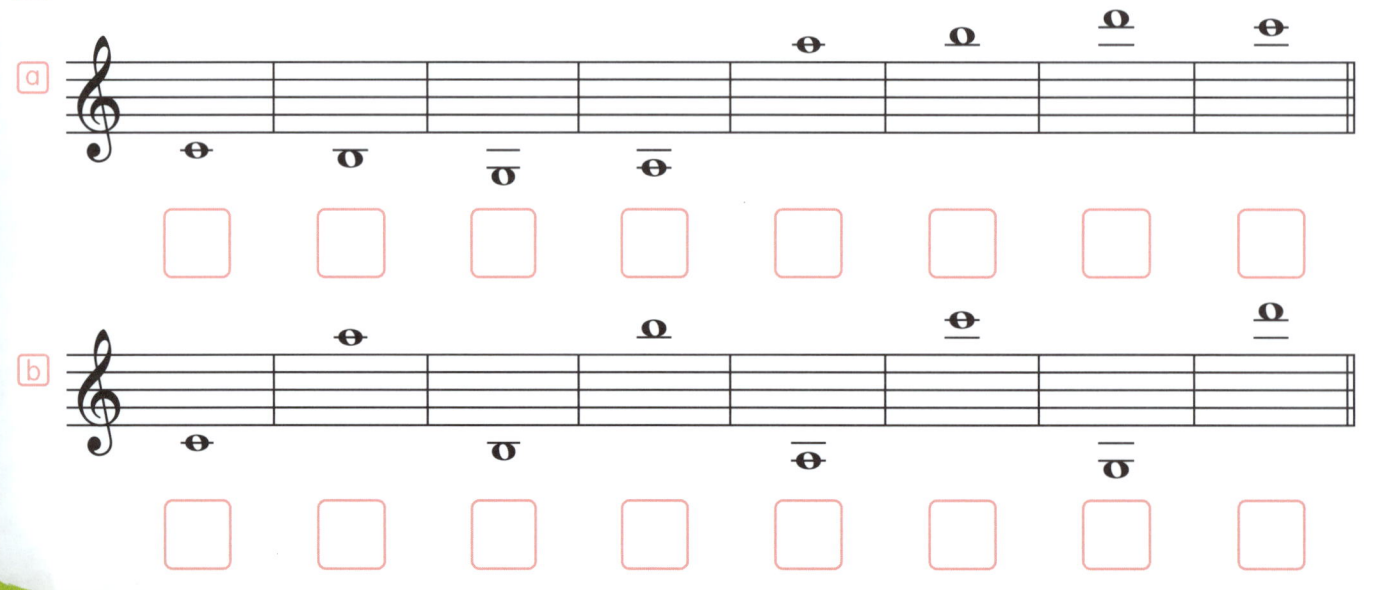

a

b

4 | Ledger Lines

2

Notes on ledger lines in bass clef

B C D E F G A B C D E F G A B C D E F

---

4 Trace and copy the notes and their letter names.

E D C B ☐ ☐ ☐ ☐   C D E F ☐ ☐ ☐ ☐

5 Fill in the missing notes as semibreves (whole notes) and their letter names.

a) ☐ ☐ ☐ ☐ ☐   b) ☐ ☐ ☐ ☐ ☐

6 Write the letter names.

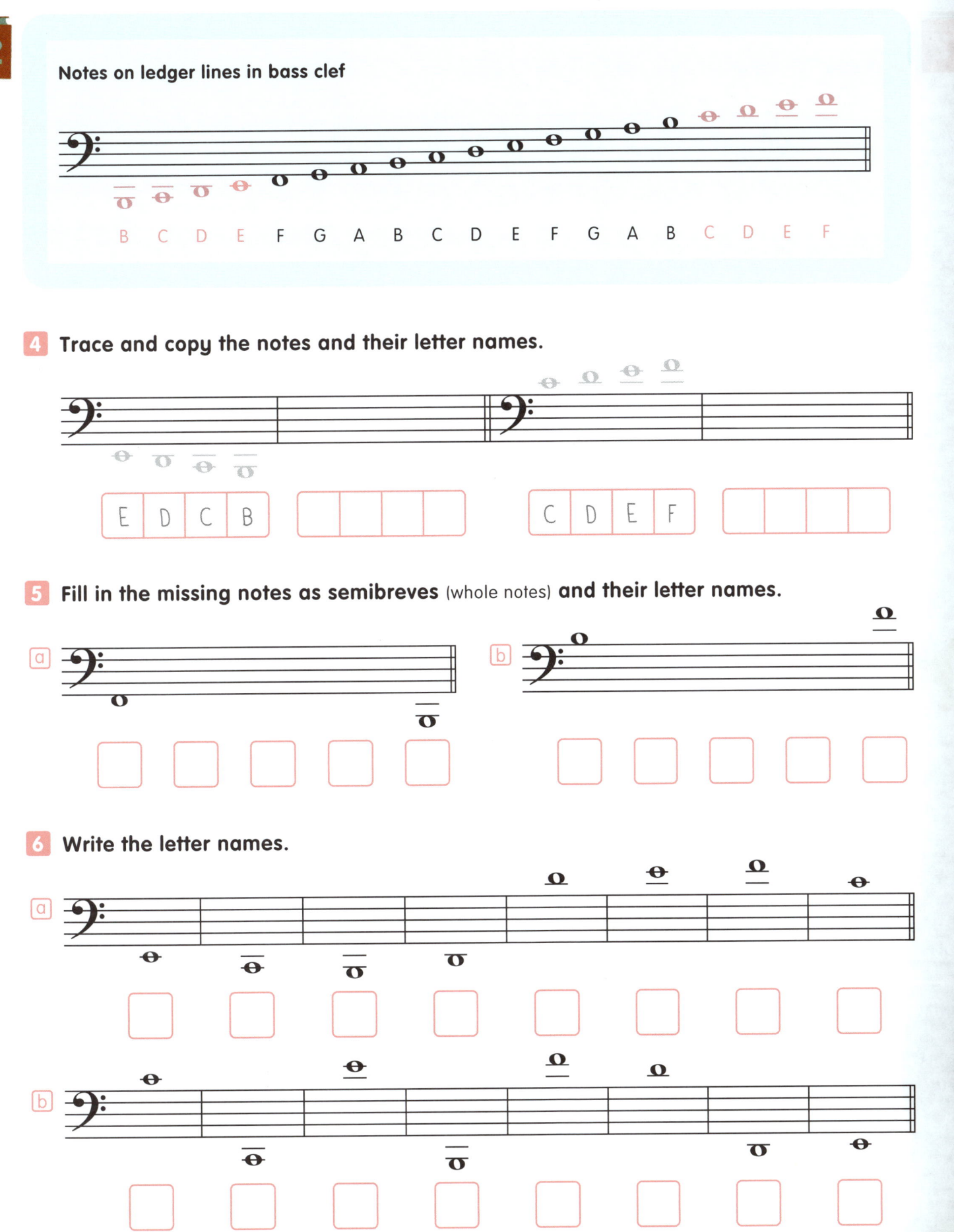

a) ☐ ☐ ☐ ☐ ☐ ☐ ☐ ☐

b) ☐ ☐ ☐ ☐ ☐ ☐ ☐

Ledger Lines | 5

3

Notes at the same pitch

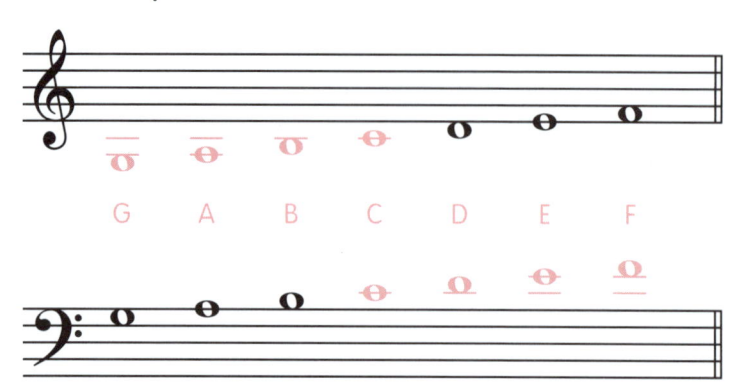

G A B C D E F

7 Write the same note(s) in the other clef.

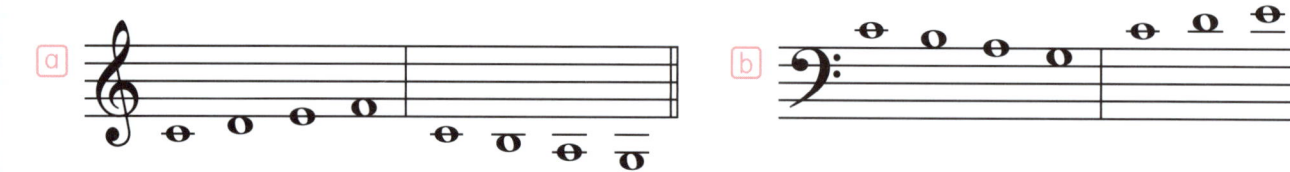

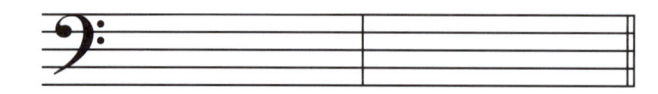

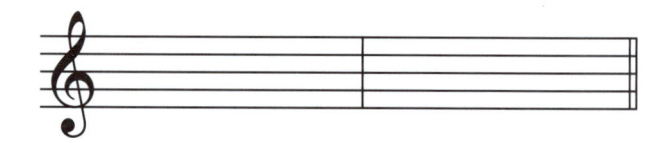

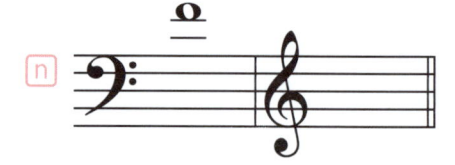

a

b

c d e

f g h

i j k

l m n

6 | Ledger Lines

8 Rewrite the melody at the same pitch in the bass clef.

9 Rewrite the melody at the same pitch in the treble clef.

10 Add clefs.

11 Write the letter name (including any sharp/flat) of each note marked *. Write the time name of the shortest/longest note.

Time name (shortest note): _____

Time name (longest note): _____

Time name (longest note): _____

Time name (shortest note): _____

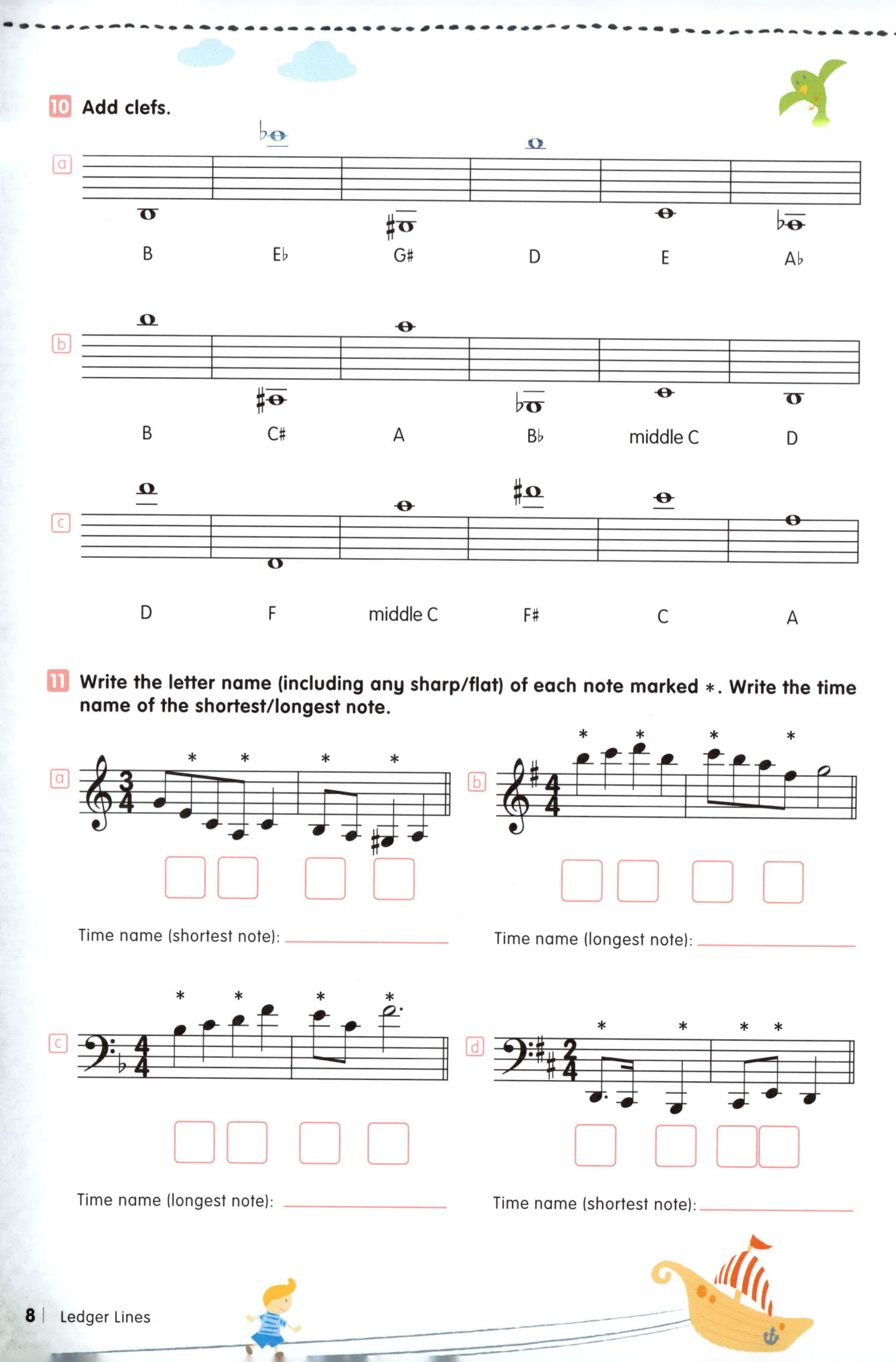

8 | Ledger Lines

Time Names and Time Values

Note values and rests

Time name	Note	Rest	Time value
semibreve (whole note)	o	▬	4
minim (half note)	𝅗𝅥	▬	2
crotchet (quarter note)	♩	𝄽	1
quaver (eighth note)	♪	𝄾	$\frac{1}{2}$
semiquaver (sixteenth note)	𝅘𝅥𝅯	𝄿	$\frac{1}{4}$

1 Write the rests and their time names.

Note	𝅗𝅥	♩	o	♩	♪
Rest					
Time name					

2 Write the notes and their time names.

Rest	𝄾	▬	𝄽	▬	𝄾
Note					
Time name					

Dotted notes

Time name	Note		Equal to:
dotted semibreve (dotted whole note)	𝅝·	𝅝 + 𝅗𝅥	𝅗𝅥 + 𝅗𝅥 + 𝅗𝅥
dotted minim (dotted half note)	𝅗𝅥·	𝅗𝅥 + 𝅘𝅥	𝅘𝅥 + 𝅘𝅥 + 𝅘𝅥
dotted crotchet (dotted quarter note)	𝅘𝅥·	𝅘𝅥 + 𝅘𝅥𝅮	𝅘𝅥𝅮 + 𝅘𝅥𝅮 + 𝅘𝅥𝅮
dotted quaver (dotted eighth note)	𝅘𝅥𝅮·	𝅘𝅥𝅮 + 𝅘𝅥𝅯	𝅘𝅥𝅯 + 𝅘𝅥𝅯 + 𝅘𝅥𝅯

3 Write the time name of the dotted note.

a) 𝅘𝅥·   b) 𝅝·   c) 𝅘𝅥𝅮·   d) 𝅗𝅥·

_____   _____   _____   _____

4 Fill in the number(s).

a) 𝅘𝅥𝅮 = ☐ 𝅘𝅥𝅯

b) 𝅘𝅥𝅮· = ☐ 𝅘𝅥𝅯

c) 𝅘𝅥 = ☐ 𝅘𝅥𝅮 = ☐ 𝅘𝅥𝅯

d) 𝅘𝅥· = ☐ 𝅘𝅥𝅮 = ☐ 𝅘𝅥𝅯

e) 𝅗𝅥 = ☐ 𝅘𝅥 = ☐ 𝅘𝅥𝅮 = ☐ 𝅘𝅥𝅯

f) 𝅗𝅥· = ☐ 𝅘𝅥 = ☐ 𝅘𝅥𝅮 = ☐ 𝅘𝅥𝅯

g) 𝅝 = ☐ 𝅗𝅥 = ☐ 𝅘𝅥 = ☐ 𝅘𝅥𝅮 = ☐ 𝅘𝅥𝅯

h) 𝅝· = ☐ 𝅗𝅥 = ☐ 𝅘𝅥 = ☐ 𝅘𝅥𝅮 = ☐ 𝅘𝅥𝅯

5 Write the time values in the order,

a) from the shortest to the longest.

𝅝   𝅗𝅥·   𝅘𝅥𝅮   𝅝·   𝅘𝅥𝅮   𝅗𝅥

☐ ☐ ☐ ☐ ☐ ☐

b) from the longest to the shortest.

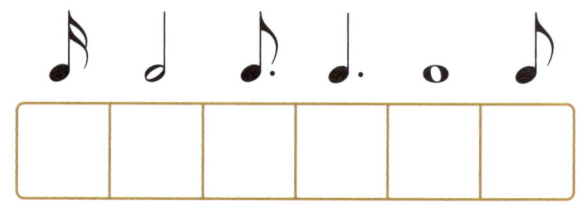

𝅘𝅥𝅯   𝅗𝅥   𝅘𝅥𝅮·   𝅗𝅥·   𝅝   𝅘𝅥𝅮

☐ ☐ ☐ ☐ ☐ ☐

10 | Time Names and Time Values

Time Signatures

Time signatures contain two numbers; $\frac{2}{2}$, $\frac{3}{2}$, $\frac{4}{2}$, $\frac{2}{4}$, $\frac{3}{4}$, $\frac{4}{4}$ and $\frac{3}{8}$.

- The **top** number shows the **number of beats** in a bar.
- The **bottom** number shows the **kind of beats** in a bar:
  2 = minim beat, **4** = crotchet beat, and **8** = quaver beat

Simple duple	Simple triple	Simple quadruple
$\frac{2}{2}$ ♩ ♩ **2** minim beats	$\frac{3}{2}$ ♩ ♩ ♩ **3** minim beats	$\frac{4}{2}$ ♩ ♩ ♩ ♩ **4** minim beats
$\frac{2}{4}$ ♩ ♩ **2** crotchet beats	$\frac{3}{4}$ ♩ ♩ ♩ **3** crotchet beats	$\frac{4}{4}$ ♩ ♩ ♩ ♩ **4** crotchet beats
	$\frac{3}{8}$ ♪ ♪ ♪ **3** quaver beats	

Notes: $\frac{2}{2}$ is sometimes written as ¢ and known as **alla breve**.

$\frac{4}{4}$ is sometimes written as C and known as **common time**.

1 Fill in notes. Complete the sentence.

a) $\frac{2}{4}$ ♩ ♩ ‖ $\frac{2}{4}$ means _2 crotchet beats in a bar_

b) $\frac{2}{2}$ ‖ $\frac{2}{2}$ means _____

c) $\frac{3}{4}$ ‖ $\frac{3}{4}$ means _____

d) $\frac{3}{2}$ ‖ $\frac{3}{2}$ means _____

e) $\frac{4}{4}$ ‖ $\frac{4}{4}$ means _____

f) $\frac{4}{2}$ ‖ $\frac{4}{2}$ means _____

g) $\frac{3}{8}$ ‖ $\frac{3}{8}$ means _____

h) ¢ ‖ ¢ means _____

2 Complete the sentence.

a) 3 in 3/4 means _____ ; 4 in 3/4 means _____

b) 4 in 4/2 means _____ ; 2 in 4/2 means _____

c) 3 in 3/8 means _____ ; 8 in 3/8 means _____

d) The top number in 2/2 means _____ ; the bottom number in 2/2 means _____ . It can also be written as _____

3 Complete the time signature.

a) 2/☐   b) 3/☐

c) 3/☐   d) 4/☐

e) 2/☐   f) 3/☐

g) 4/☐   h) 2/☐

4 Add the time signature.

a)   b)

c)   d)

e)   f)

12 | Time Signatures

5 Add the missing bar-lines.

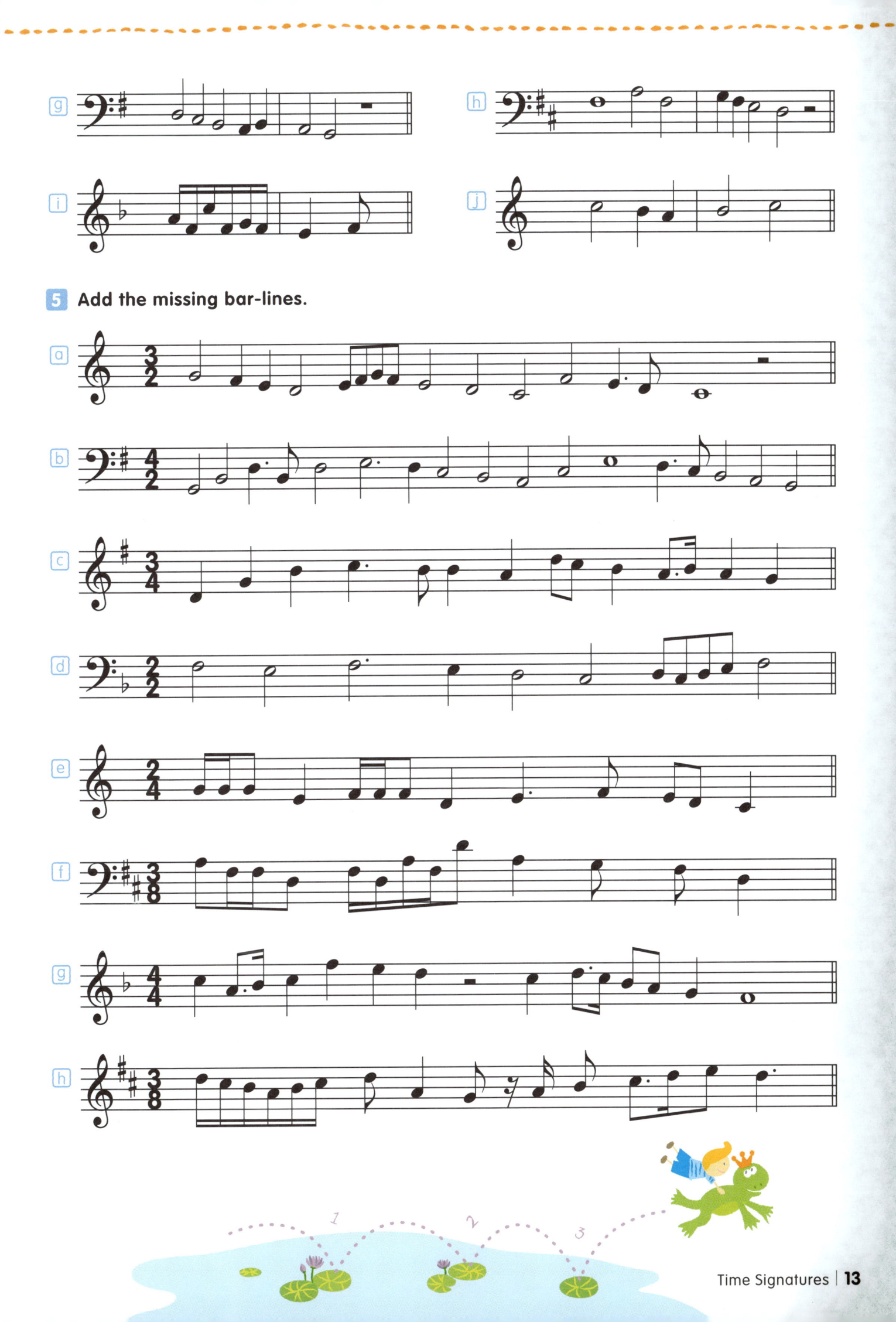

6 **Rewrite the following in notes and rests of twice the value. Name the time signature (e.g. duple, triple, quadruple) for both.**

Time: _____

Time: _____

Time: _____

7 Rewrite the following in notes and rests of half the value. Name the time signature (e.g. duple, triple, quadruple) for both.

Time: _____

Time: _____

Time: _____

Triplets

A triplet is a group of 3 notes played in the time of 2. A triplet can include rests and notes with different values.

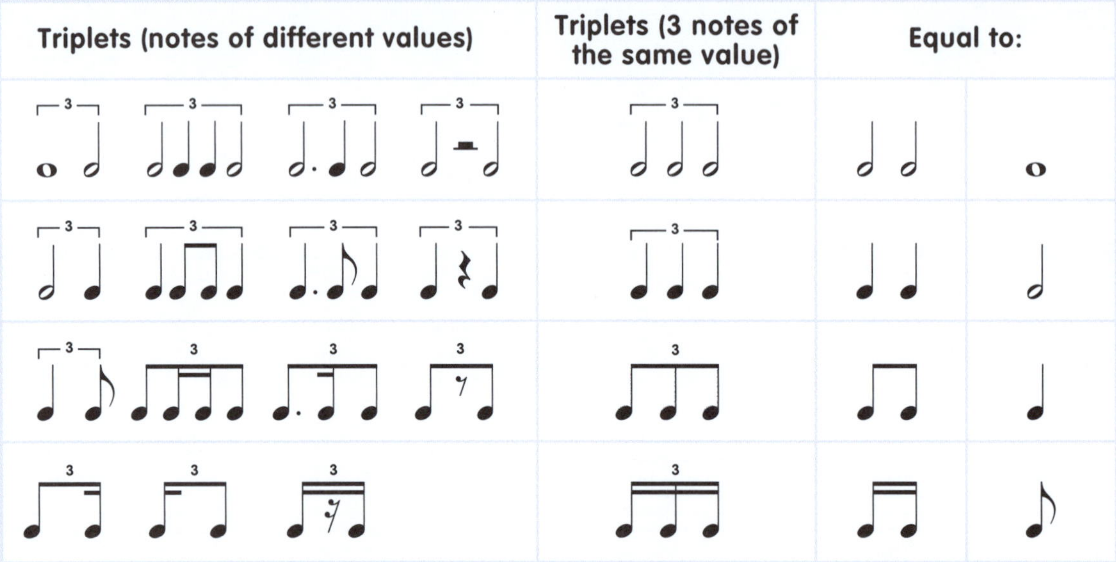

Triplets (notes of different values)	Triplets (3 notes of the same value)	Equal to:	

1 Write 1 note which is equal to each triplet.

a) are played in the time of a ☐

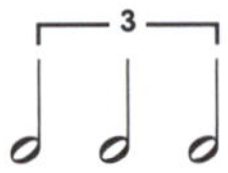

b) are played in the time of a ☐

c) are played in the time of a ☐

d) are played in the time of a ☐

e) are played in the time of a ☐

f) are played in the time of a ☐

g) are played in the time of a ☐

h) are played in the time of a ☐

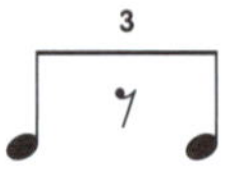

i) are played in the time of a ☐

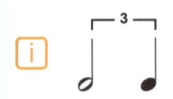

j) are played in the time of a ☐

16 | Triplets

2 Write 1 triplet which is equal to each note.

a) o =

b) ♩ =

c) ♩ =

d) ♪ =

3 Add the time signature.

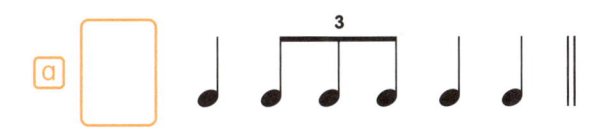

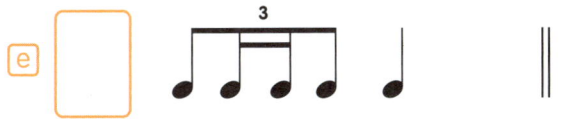

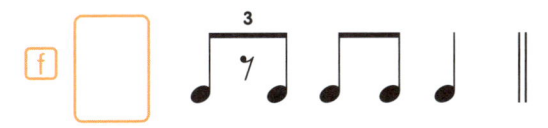

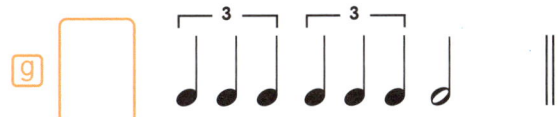

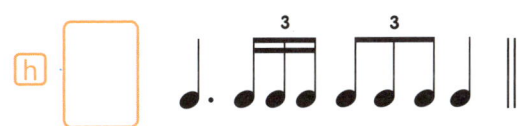

4 Add 1 rest at each ∗.

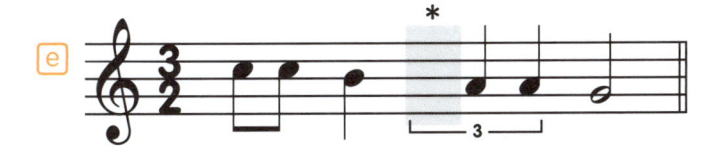

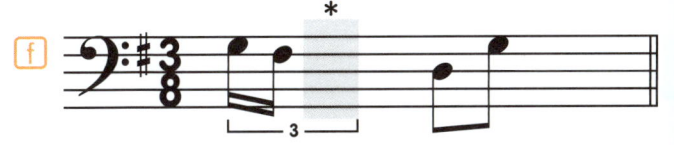

5 Add the missing bar-lines.

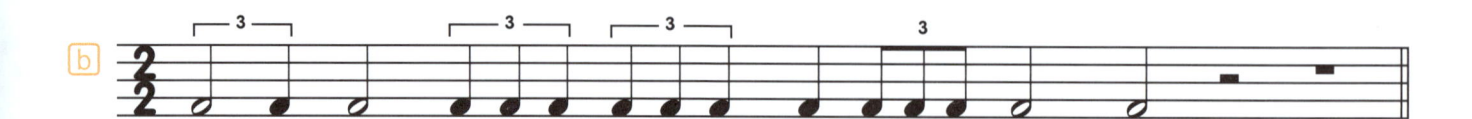

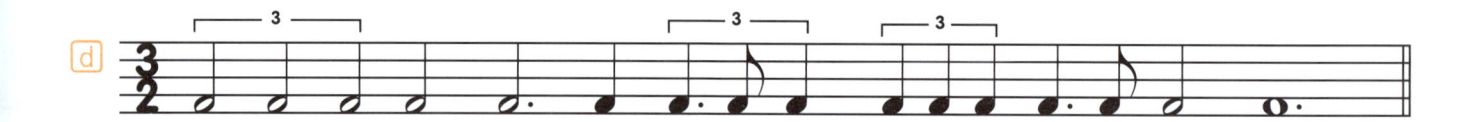

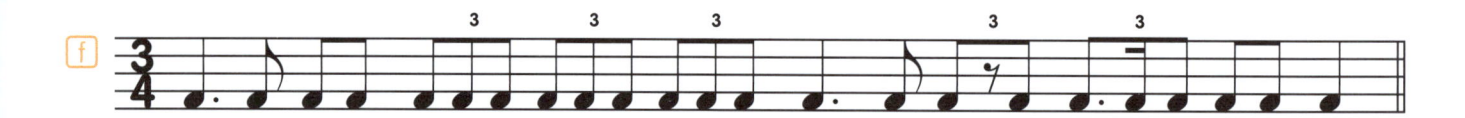

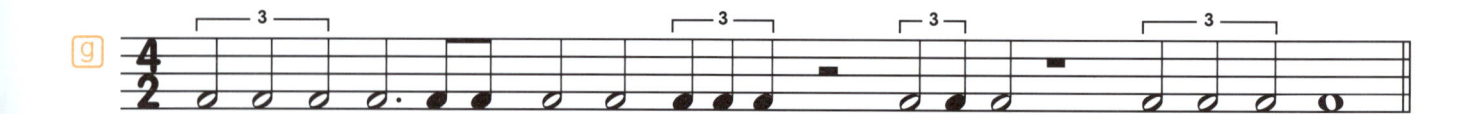

6 Answer the questions.

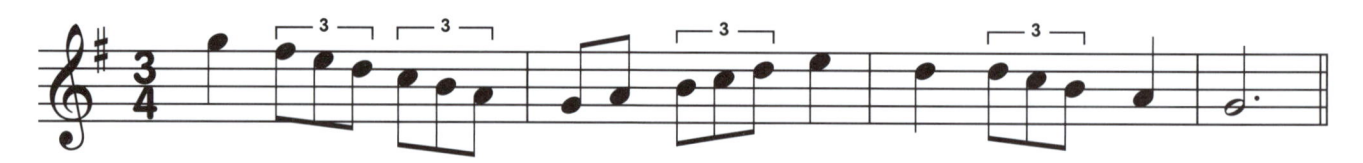

a) How many bars contain a triplet? _____

b) The rhythm ♪♪♪ occurs _____ times.

c) The triplet ♪♪♪ in bar 2 means 3 quavers (eighth-notes) in the time of a _____.

18 | Triplets

Grouping of Notes

Grouping of notes

- In a bar, use single notes wherever possible, do not use ties.

1 Rewrite the music correctly.

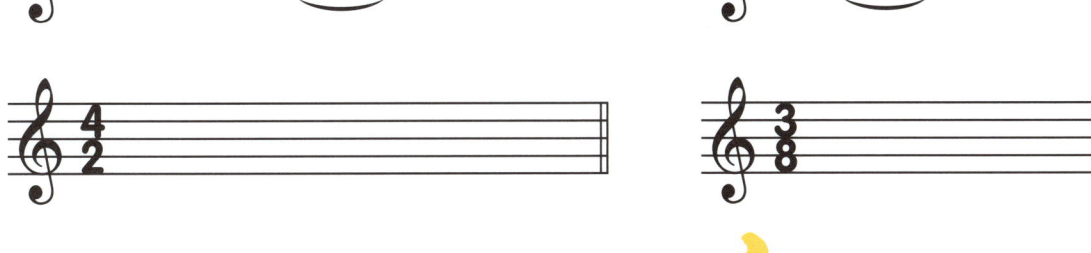

- In $\frac{2}{4}$, $\frac{3}{4}$ and $\frac{4}{4}$, beam notes in crotchet beats.

- In $\frac{2}{2}$, $\frac{3}{2}$ and $\frac{4}{2}$, beam notes in minim beats.

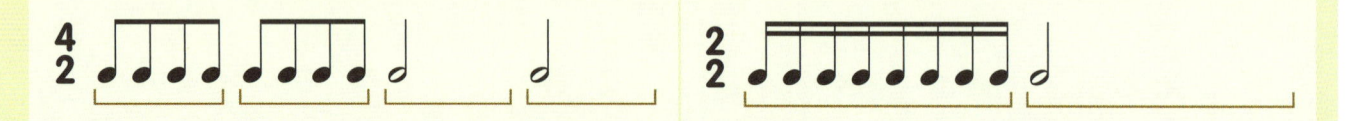

- In $\frac{3}{8}$, beam all quavers and/or semiquavers to make a bar.

- Beam over rests.

Stem direction

Find the direction by:
- the majority of the notes above/below the middle.

- the note furthest from the middle.

20 | Grouping of Notes

2 Mark any mistakes in the grouping of notes. Group/beam the notes correctly.

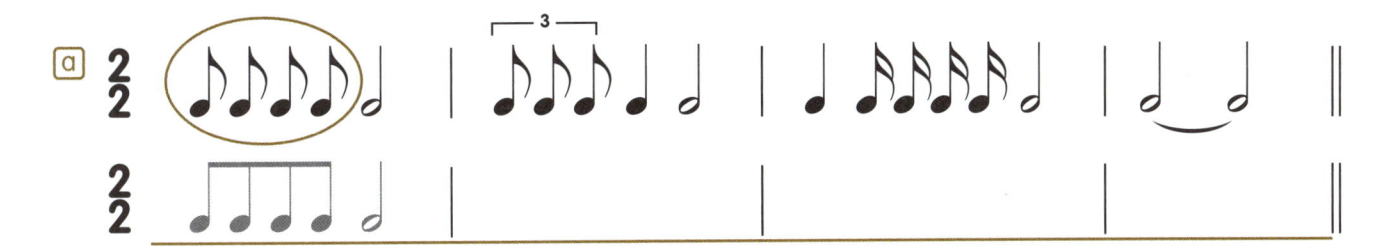

3 Mark any mistakes in the grouping of notes. Rewrite the melody correctly.

Grouping of Rests

Grouping of rests

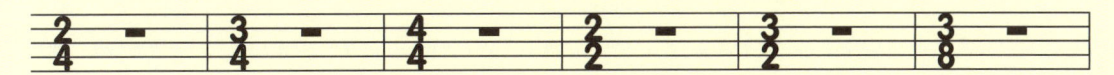

- In $\frac{2}{4}, \frac{3}{4}, \frac{4}{4}, \frac{3}{2}, \frac{2}{2}$ and $\frac{3}{8}$, use a semibreve rest (whole bar rest) to fill a bar.

- Use a rest for every beat.

- In a bar of 4 beats, use a 2-beat rest for the first 2 beats/the last 2 beats, do not use a 2-beat rest in the middle.

1 Use ⊓ to mark each beat division. Add the correct rest(s) at each ∗.

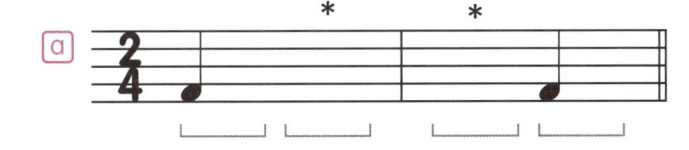

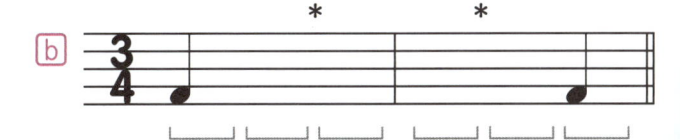

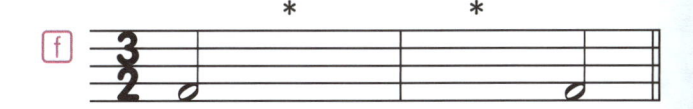

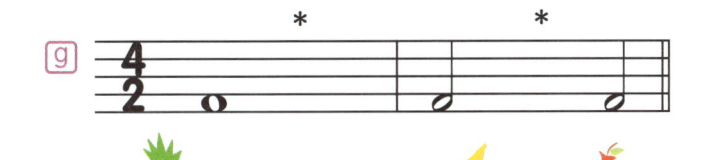

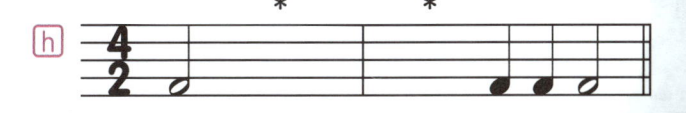

- When a silence is less than a beat, use a rest for every subdivision of the beat.

- When a silence is more than a beat, use as few rests as possible.

24 | Grouping of Rests

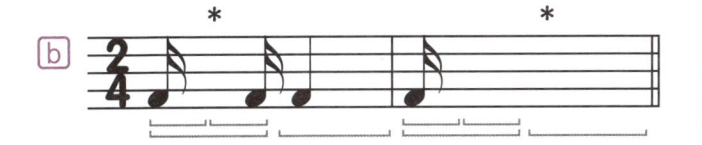

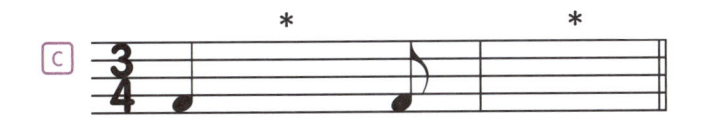

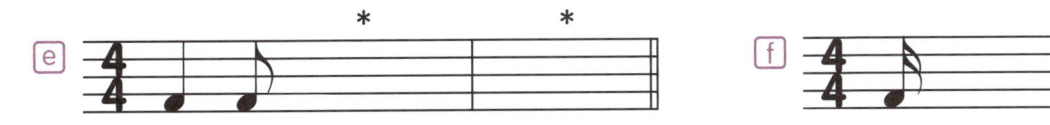

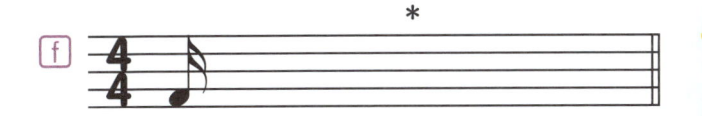

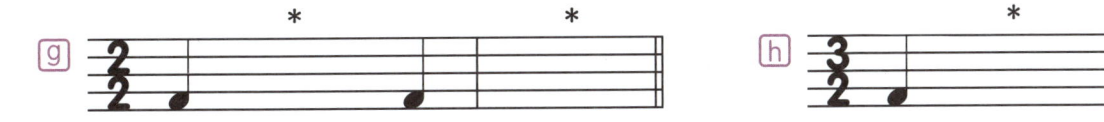

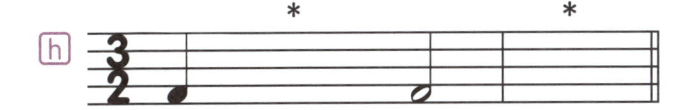

2 Use ⌐ to mark each beat division. Add the correct rest(s) at each *.

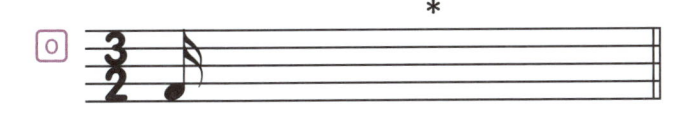

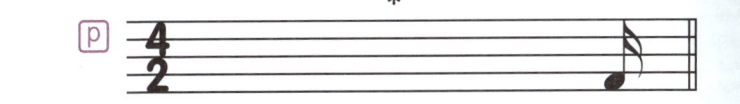

3 Use ⌐ to mark each beat division. Add the correct rest(s) at each *.

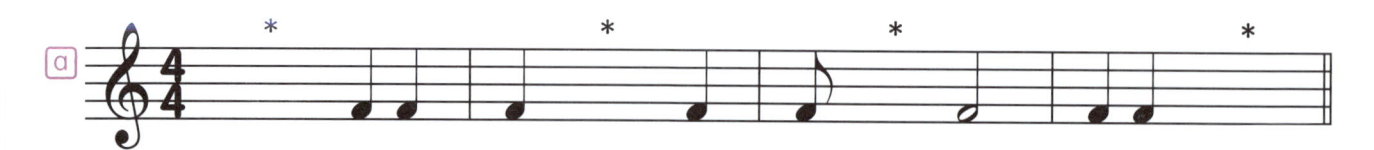

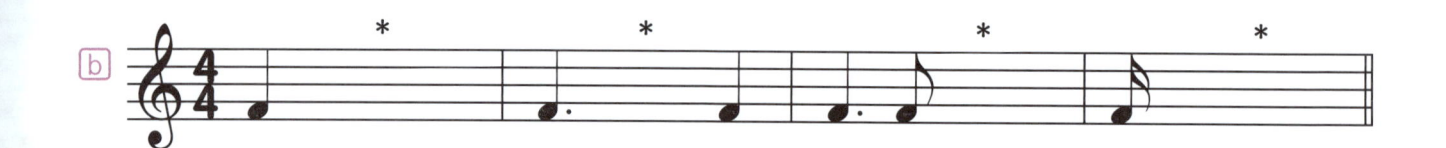

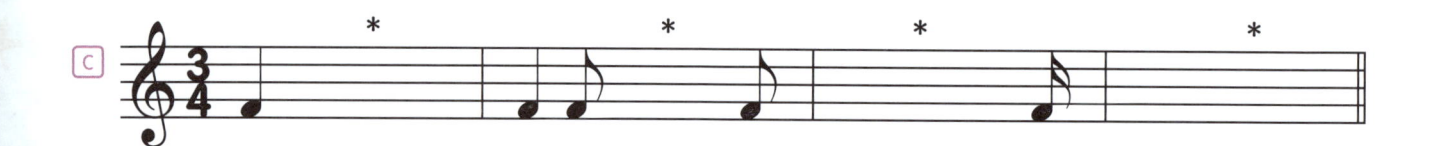

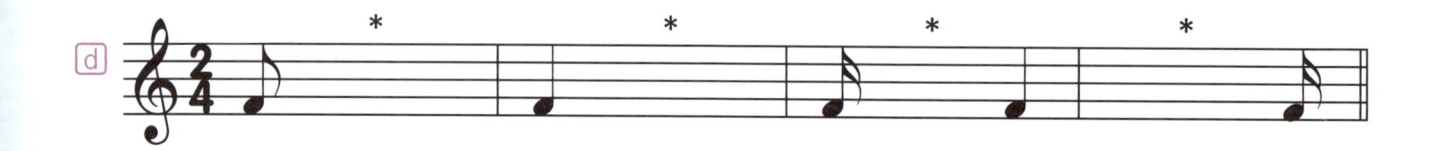

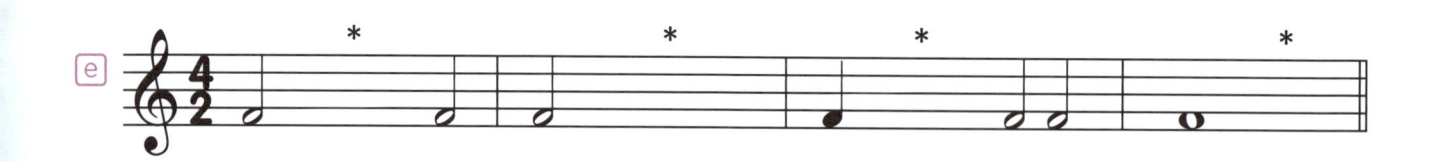

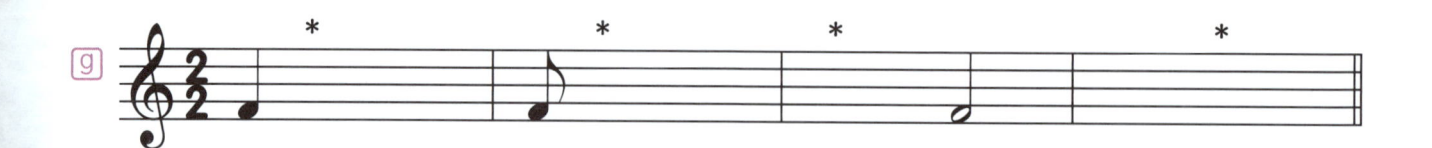

26 | Grouping of Rests

4 Mark any mistake in the grouping of notes and rests. Rewrite the melody correctly.

The Scales and Key Signatures of A, B♭ and E♭ Major

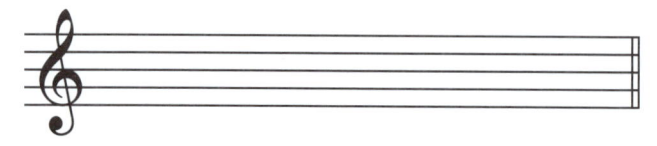

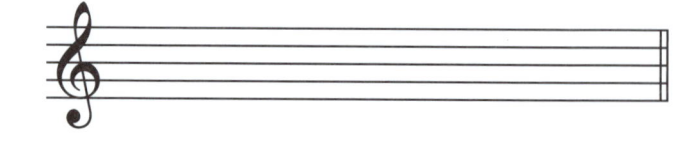

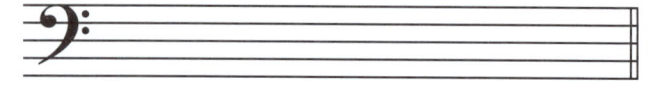

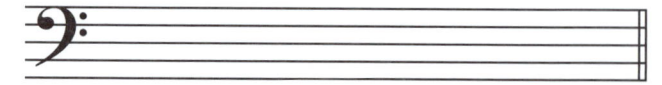

1 Write the letter names of the notes that make up the scale.

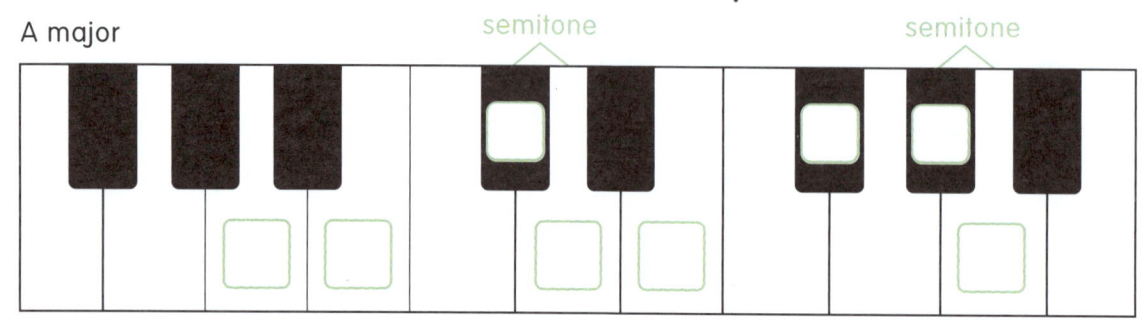

A major

2 Add sharps/flats (where necessary). Mark the semitones with ⌐⌐.

a) A major, ascending

b) A major, descending

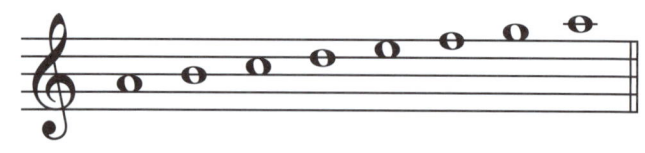

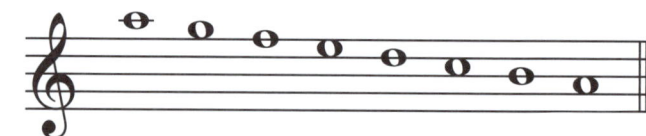

3 Copy the clefs, key signature and key name.

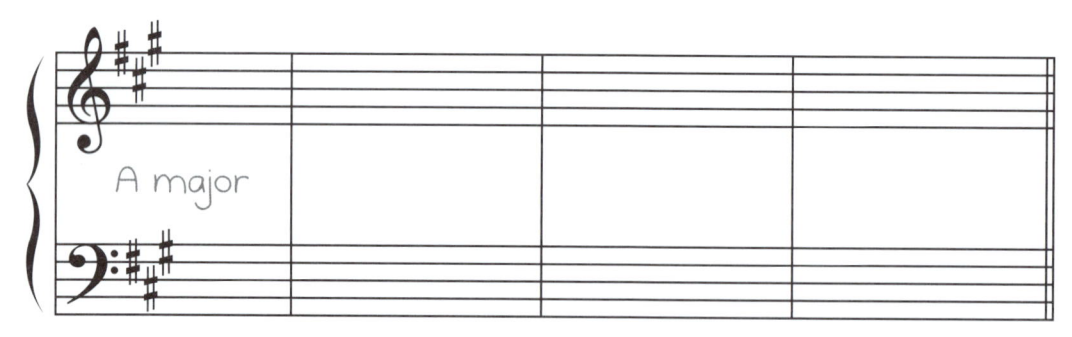

A major

4 Write the scale in semibreves (whole notes), using a key signature.

a) A major, ascending

b) A major, descending

28 | The Scales and Key Signatures of A, B♭ and E♭ Major

5 Write the letter names of the notes that make up the scale.

B♭ major

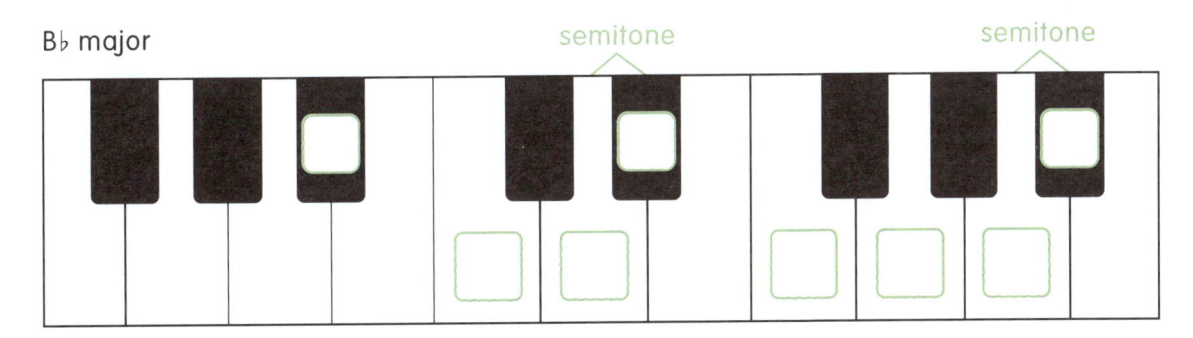

6 Add sharps/flats (where necessary). Mark the semitones with ⌐┐.

a) B♭ major, ascending

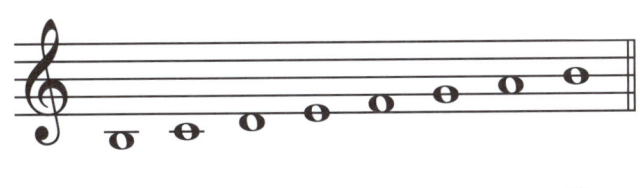

b) B♭ major, descending

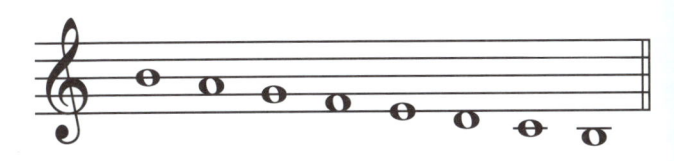

7 Copy the clefs, key signature and key name.

B♭ major

8 Write the scale in semibreves (whole notes), using a key signature.

a) B♭ major, ascending

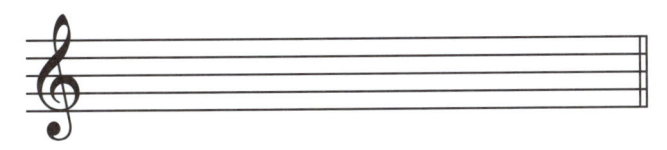

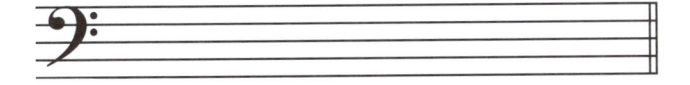

b) B♭ major, descending

The Scales and Key Signatures of A, B♭ and E♭ Major | 29

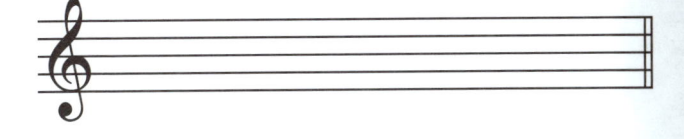

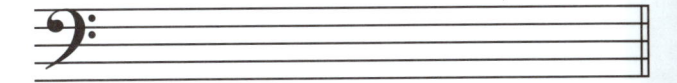

9 Write the letter names of the notes that make up the scale.

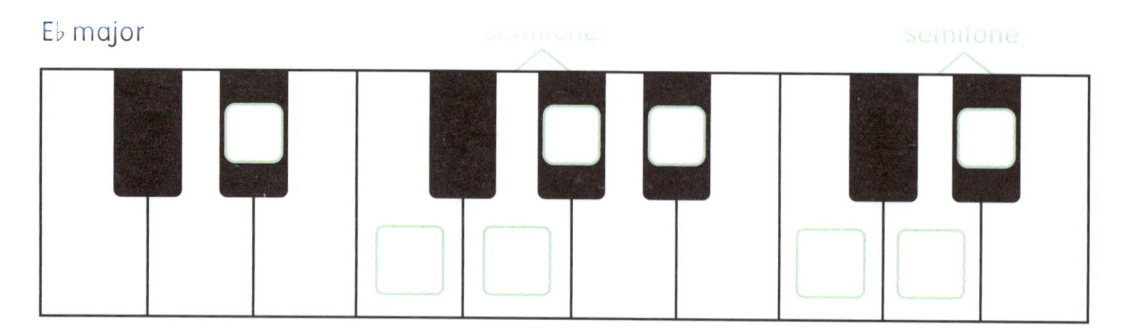

E♭ major

10 Add sharps/flats (where necessary). Mark the semitones with ⌐⌐.

a E♭ major, ascending

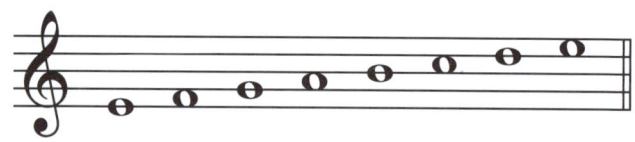

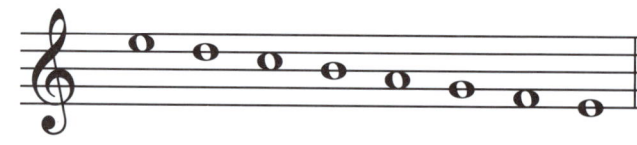

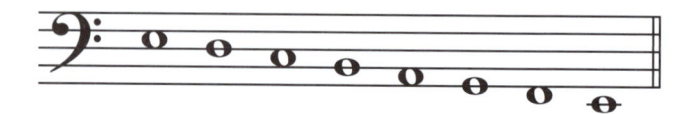

b E♭ major, descending

11 Copy the clefs, key signature and key name.

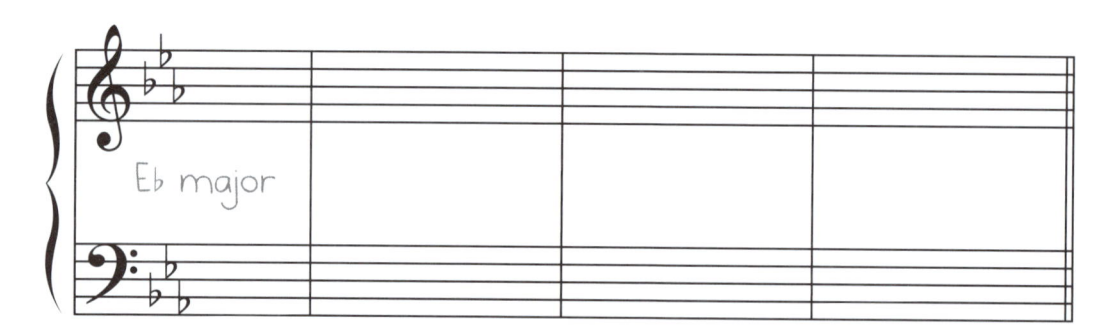

E♭ major

12 Write the scale in semibreves (whole notes), using a key signature.

a E♭ major, ascending

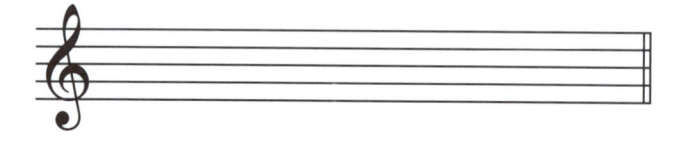

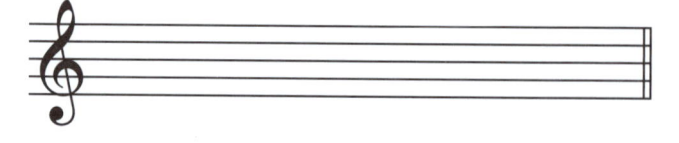

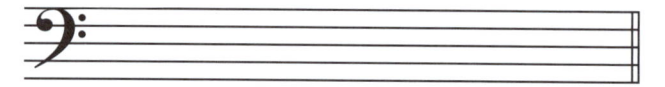

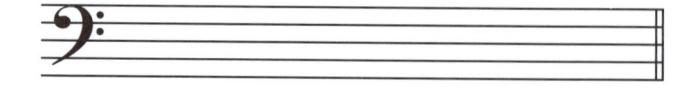

b E♭ major, descending

30 | The Scales and Key Signatures of A, B♭ and E♭ Major

Building key signatures

The **circle of 5ths** is used to build the key signatures for keys that contain sharp/flat notes.
- As move right from C major, 1 new sharp is added to the new key.
- As move left from C major, 1 new flat is added to the new key.

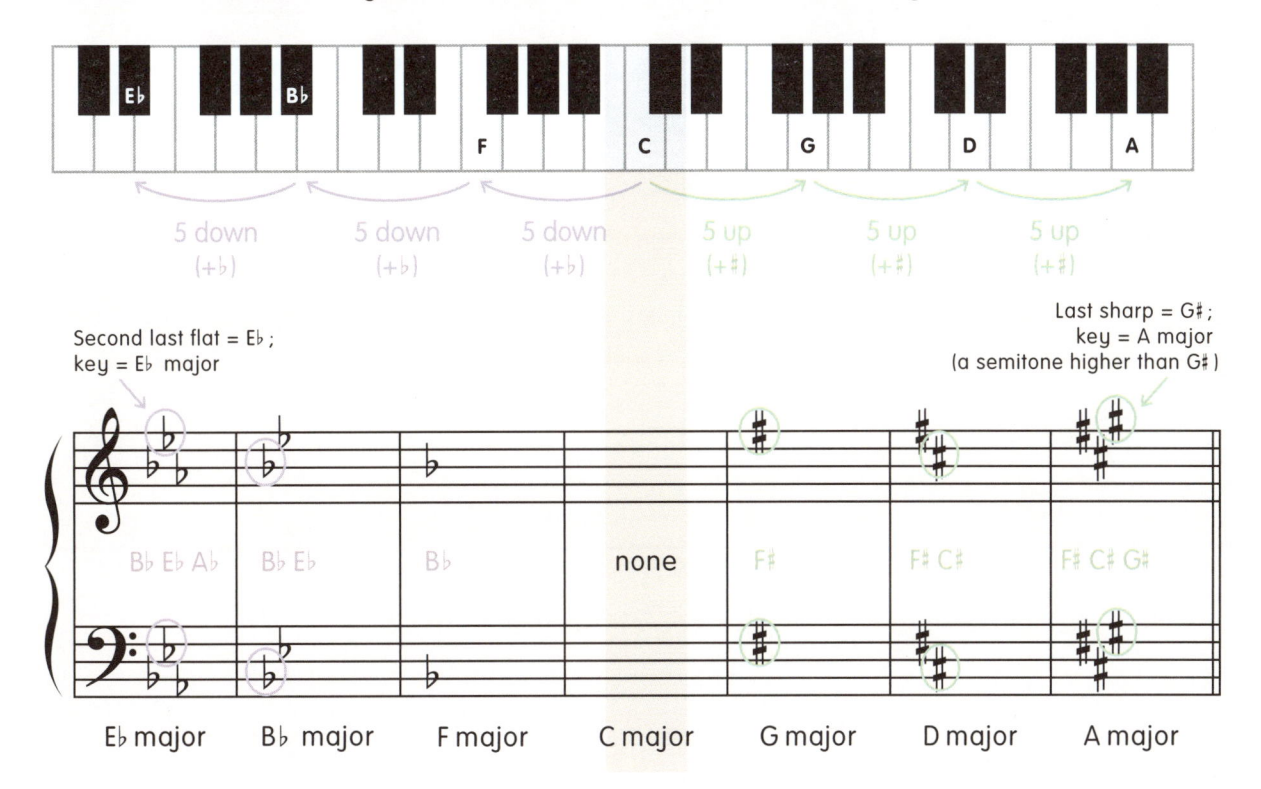

Keyboard: E♭ — B♭ — F — C — G — D — A

5 down (+♭) | 5 down (+♭) | 5 down (+♭) | 5 up (+♯) | 5 up (+♯) | 5 up (+♯)

Second last flat = E♭ ; key = E♭ major

Last sharp = G♯ ; key = A major (a semitone higher than G♯)

E♭ major	B♭ major	F major	C major	G major	D major	A major
B♭ E♭ A♭	B♭ E♭	B♭	none	F♯	F♯ C♯	F♯ C♯ G♯

Naming a major key
The name of the sharp key is one semitone higher than the last sharp.
The name of the flat key is the second last flat.

13 Circle the last sharp and name the note above it.

a) ____ major   b) ____ major   c) ____ major   d) ____ major

14 Circle and name the second last flat.

a) ____ major   b) ____ major   c) ____ major   d) ____ major

The Scales and Key Signatures of A, B♭ and E♭ Major | 31

15 Name the major key.

a, b, 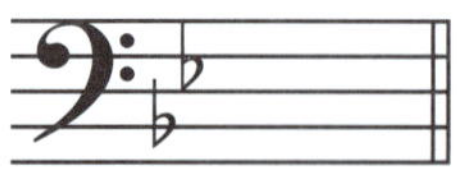 c,  d

e,  f,  g,  h

i,  j,  k,  l

16 Name the sharps/flats and write the key signature of the key.

a G major: F#

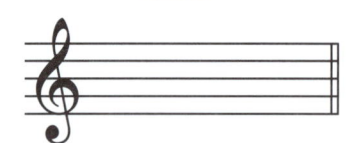

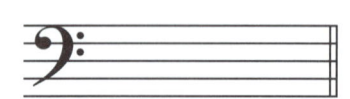

b D major: ☐ ☐

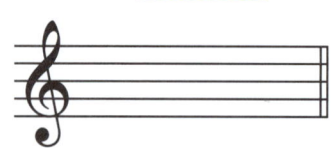

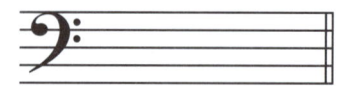

c A major: ☐ ☐ ☐

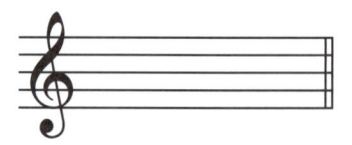

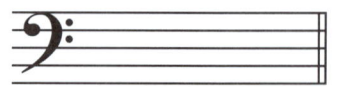

d F major: ☐

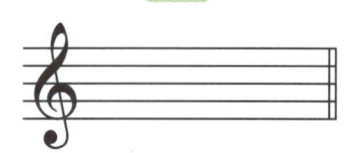

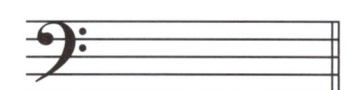

e B♭ major: ☐ ☐

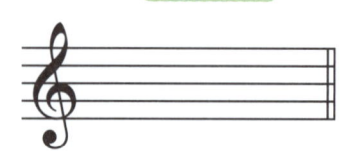

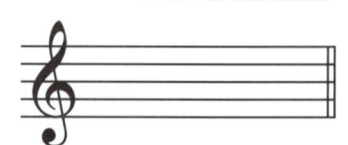

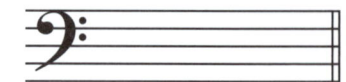

f E♭ major: ☐ ☐ ☐

17 Add the clef and key signature to make the scale.

a) A major

b) B♭ major

c) E♭ major

d) F major

e) G major

18 Add the clef and any sharps/flats to make the scale. (Do not use a key signature.)

a) B♭ major

b) E♭ major

c) A major

d) D major

e) G major

The Scales and Key Signatures of A, B♭ and E♭ Major

19 Write the scale in semibreves (whole notes), using a key signature.

a) B♭ major descending

b) A major ascending

c) E♭ major descending

d) F major ascending

e) G major descending

20 Write the scale in semibreves (whole notes). (Do not use a key signature, but add any sharps/flats.)

a) A major descending

b) B♭ major ascending

c) E♭ major ascending

d) D major descending

e) G major ascending

34 | The Scales and Key Signatures of A, B♭ and E♭ Major

1

Rewriting melodies with or without a key signature

From without to with a key signature
- List the sharps/flats of the key and cross them out in the melody.
- Circle out any accidentals (sharps/flats NOT found in the key).

D major: F♯ C♯

- Write a key signature with the sharps/flats of the key.
- Copy the melody, keeping any accidentals.

2

Rewrite the melody using the correct key signature. (Leave out the sharps/flats of the key, but keep any accidentals.)

(a) B♭ major

(b) A major

(c) E♭ major

The Scales and Key Signatures of A, B♭ and E♭ Major | 35

2 From with to without a key signature

- List the sharps/flats of the key and place a sharp/flat sign above each sharpened/flatted note.
- Circle out any accidentals.

E♭ major: **B♭ E♭ A♭**

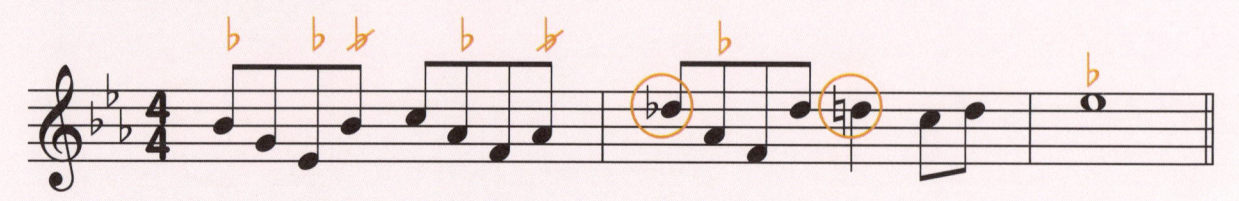

- Copy the melody, adding the sharps/flats of the key and keeping any accidentals.

22 Rewrite the melody without using a key signature. (Add the sharps/flats of the key, and keep any accidentals.)

a A major

b E♭ major

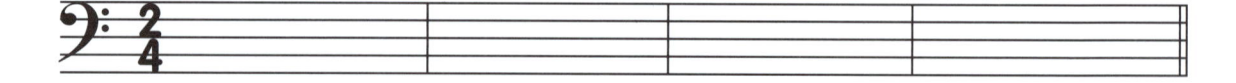

c B♭ major

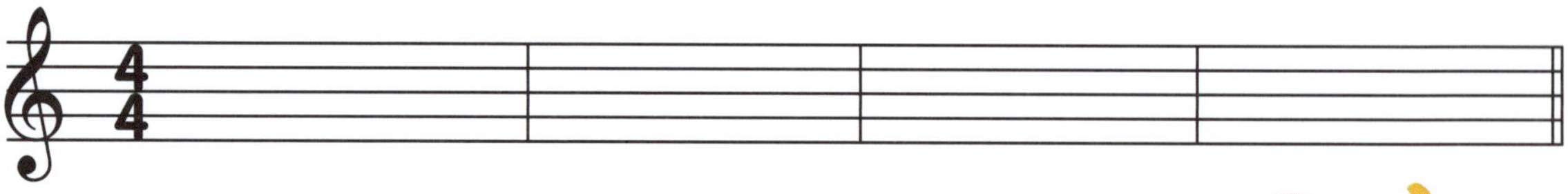

The Scales and Key Signatures of A, E and D Minor

Minor scales

Every major scale has a relative minor scale, which uses the same notes as the major scale, but starts on the 6th degree of the major scale. There are 3 types of minor scales: **natural minor**, **harmonic minor**, and **melodic minor**.

Natural minor
Natural minor scale uses the same notes as its relative major scale.

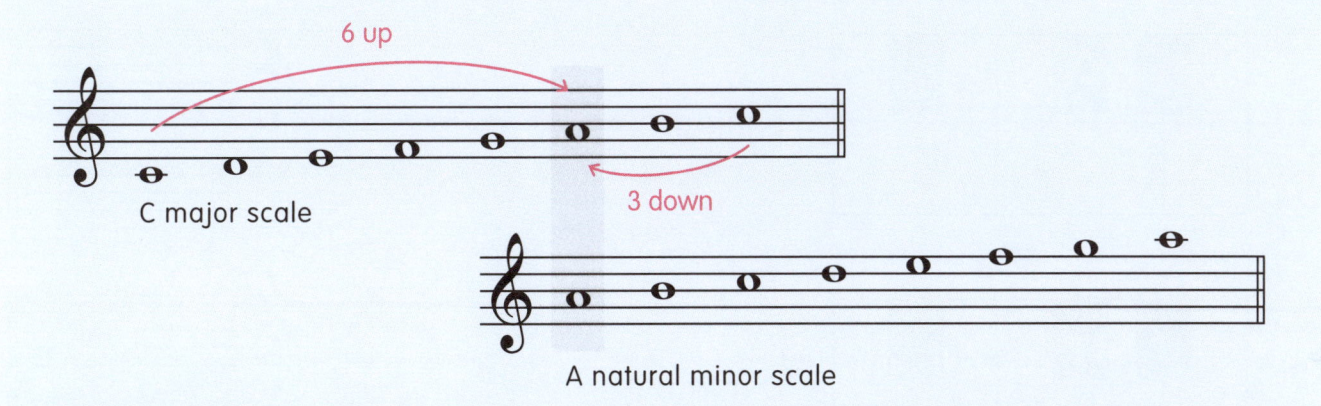

C major scale

A natural minor scale

Harmonic minor
Harmonic minor scale uses the same notes as its relative major scale, except the 7th scale degree is raised.

A *harmonic* minor, ascending

A *harmonic* minor, descending

Melodic minor
Melodic minor scale uses the same notes as its relative major scale, except the 6th and 7th scale degrees are raised as the scale ascends, but return to the natural minor scale as it descends.

A *melodic* minor, ascending

A *melodic* minor, descending

1 Name the relative major of each minor and write the key signature for both.

Relation between minor and major	Minor	Major (3 semitones from minor)	Key signature
A minor → C major	A minor	C major	
E minor → G major	E minor		
D minor → F major	D minor		

2 Name the key.

a. ☐ minor
b. ☐ minor
c. ☐ minor
d. ☐ minor
e. ☐ minor
f. ☐ minor
g. ☐ minor
h. ☐ minor

38 | The Scales and Key Signatures of A, E and D Minor

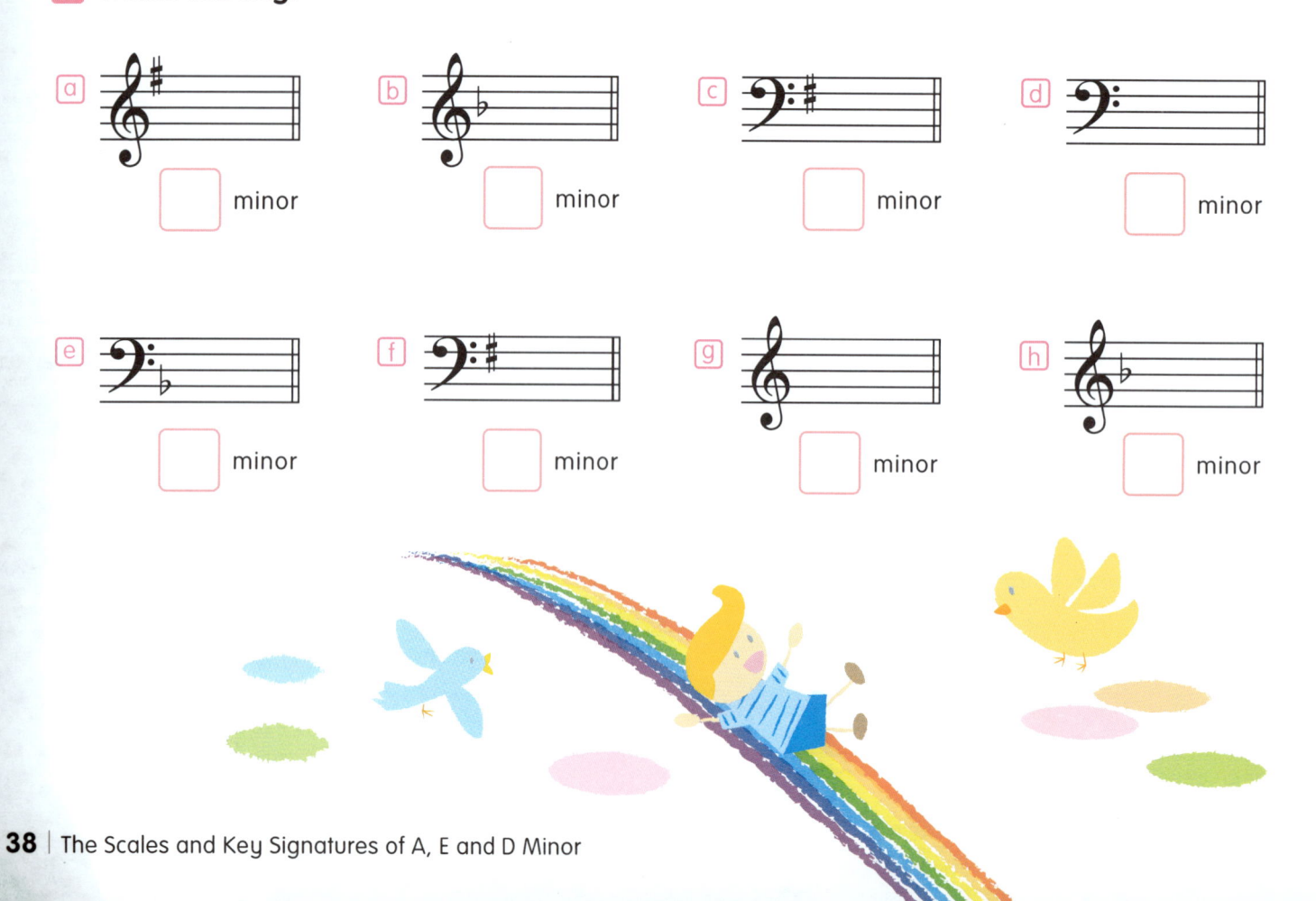

3 Add any necessary sharps/flats and sharpen the 7th note to make the harmonic scale. Mark the semitones with ⌐.

a) A harmonic minor, ascending

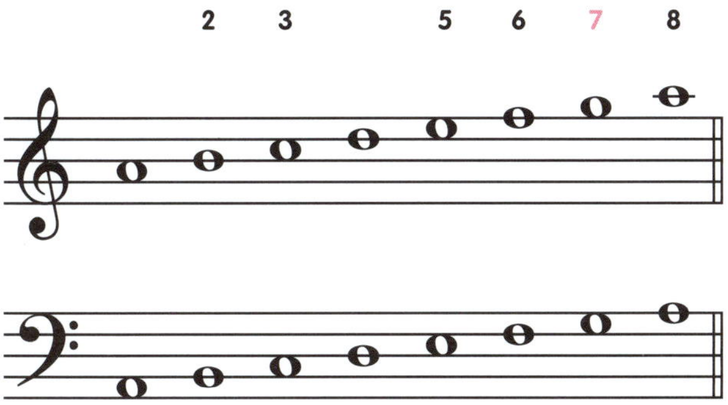

b) A harmonic minor, descending

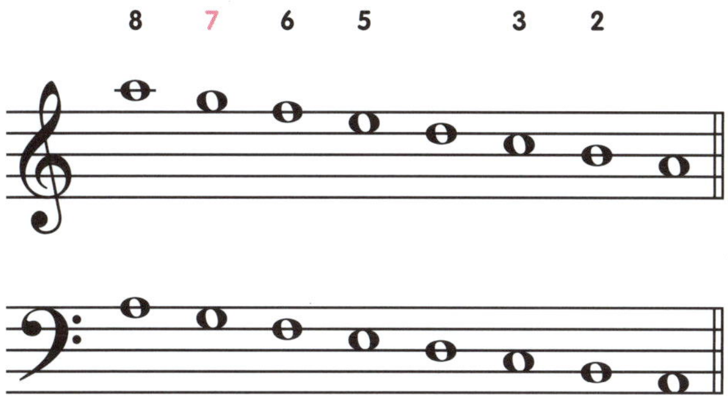

c) E harmonic minor, ascending

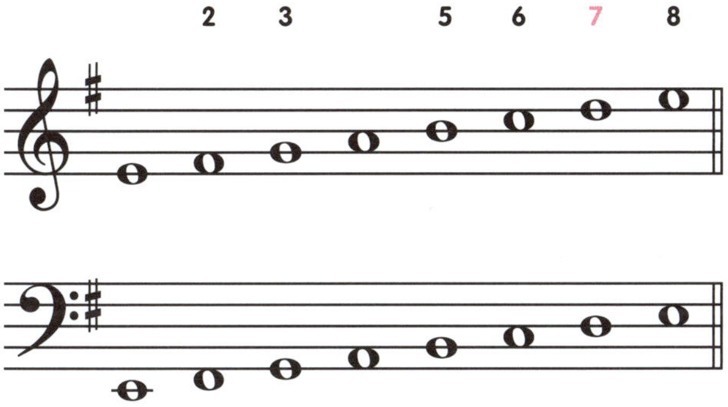

d) E harmonic minor, descending

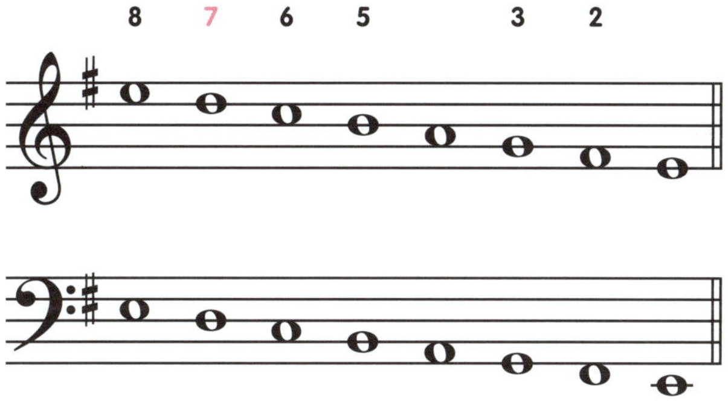

e) D harmonic minor, ascending

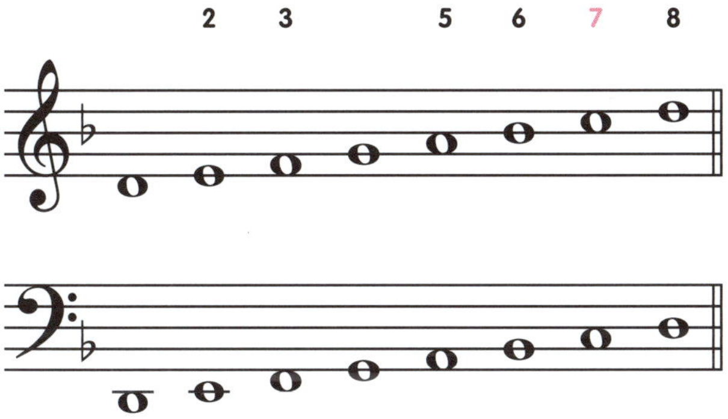

f) D harmonic minor, descending

The Scales and Key Signatures of A, E and D Minor | 39

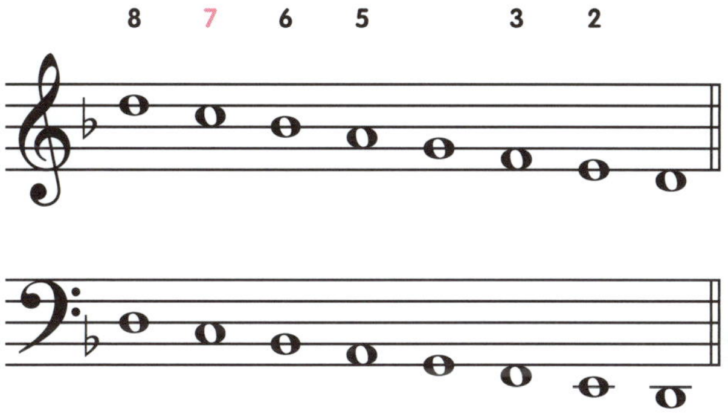

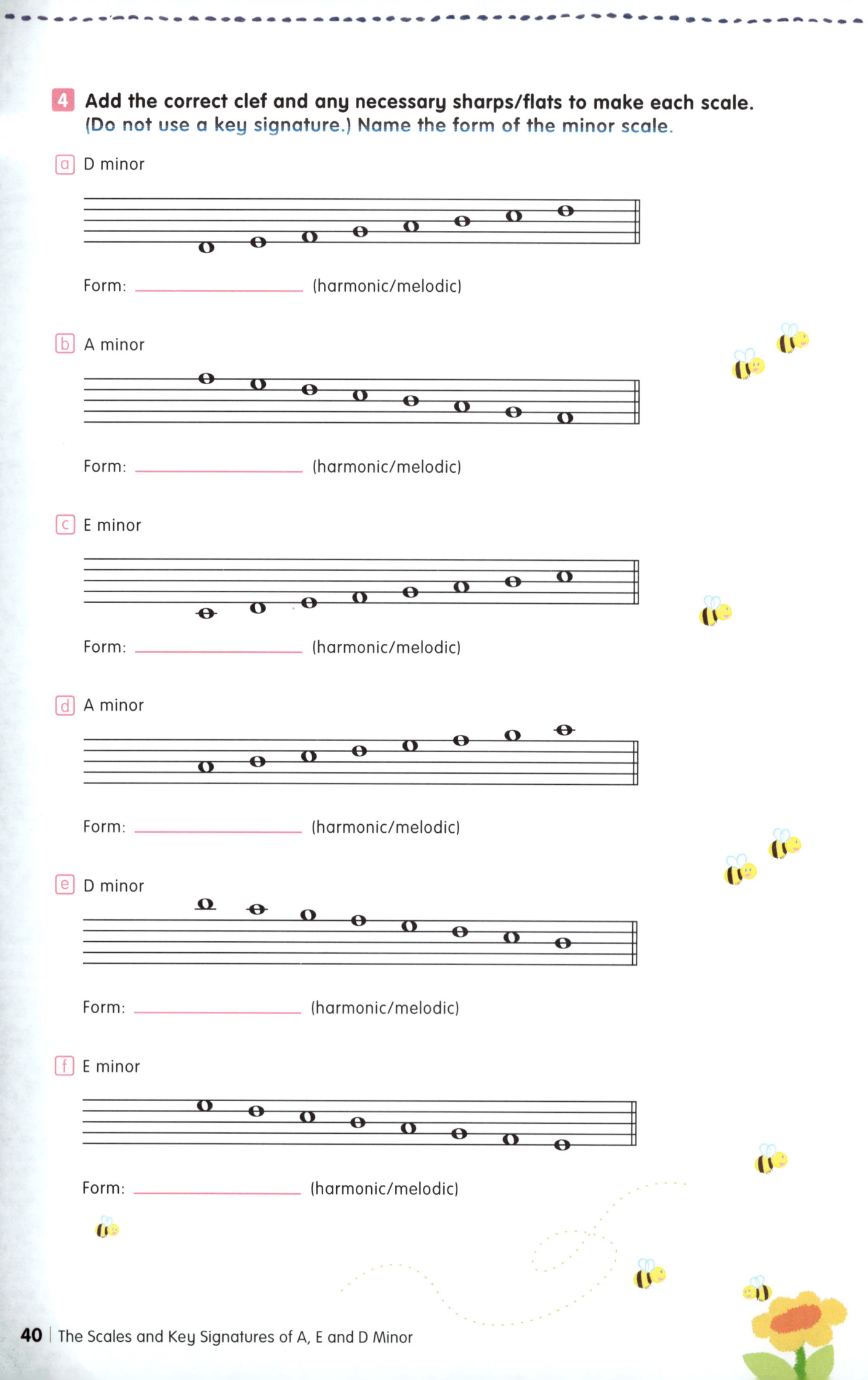

4 **Add the correct clef and any necessary sharps/flats to make each scale.** (Do not use a key signature.) Name the form of the minor scale.

a) D minor

Form: _____ (harmonic/melodic)

b) A minor

Form: _____ (harmonic/melodic)

c) E minor

Form: _____ (harmonic/melodic)

d) A minor

Form: _____ (harmonic/melodic)

e) D minor

Form: _____ (harmonic/melodic)

f) E minor

Form: _____ (harmonic/melodic)

5 **Write the scale in semibreves** (whole-notes)**, using a key signature. Name the form of the minor scale.**

a) E minor, ascending

Form: _____ (harmonic/melodic)

b) A minor, descending

Form: _____ (harmonic/melodic)

c) D minor, descending

Form: _____ (harmonic/melodic)

d) A minor, ascending

Form: _____ (harmonic/melodic)

e) D minor, ascending

Form: _____ (harmonic/melodic)

f) E minor, descending

Form: _____ (harmonic/melodic)

6 **Write the scale in semibreves** (whole-notes)**, without using a key signature but adding any necessary sharps/flats. Name the form of the minor scale.**

a D minor, ascending

Form: _____ (harmonic/melodic)

b E minor, descending

Form: _____ (harmonic/melodic)

c A minor, descending

Form: _____ (harmonic/melodic)

d D minor, descending

Form: _____ (harmonic/melodic)

e A minor, ascending

Form: _____ (harmonic/melodic)

f E minor, ascending

Form: _____ (harmonic/melodic)

Tonic Triads

A tonic triad consists of 3 notes: the 1st, 3rd and 5th degrees of the scale.

C major   A minor

Note: The key of C major and A minor has no sharps or flats.

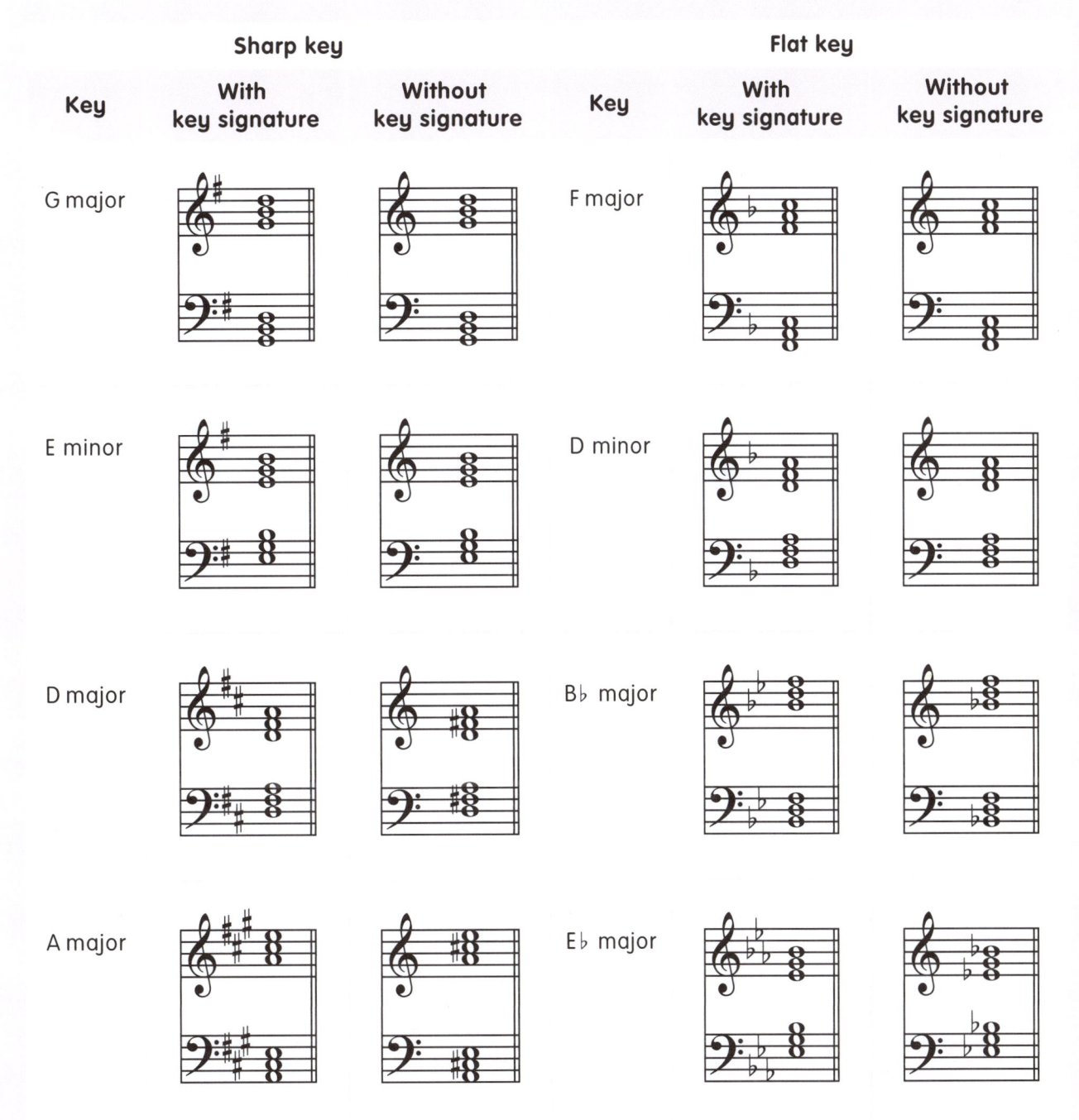

Key	Sharp key — With key signature	Without key signature	Key	Flat key — With key signature	Without key signature
G major			F major		
E minor			D minor		
D major			B♭ major		
A major			E♭ major		

Tonic Triads | 43

1 Write the letter names and name the key of the tonic triad.

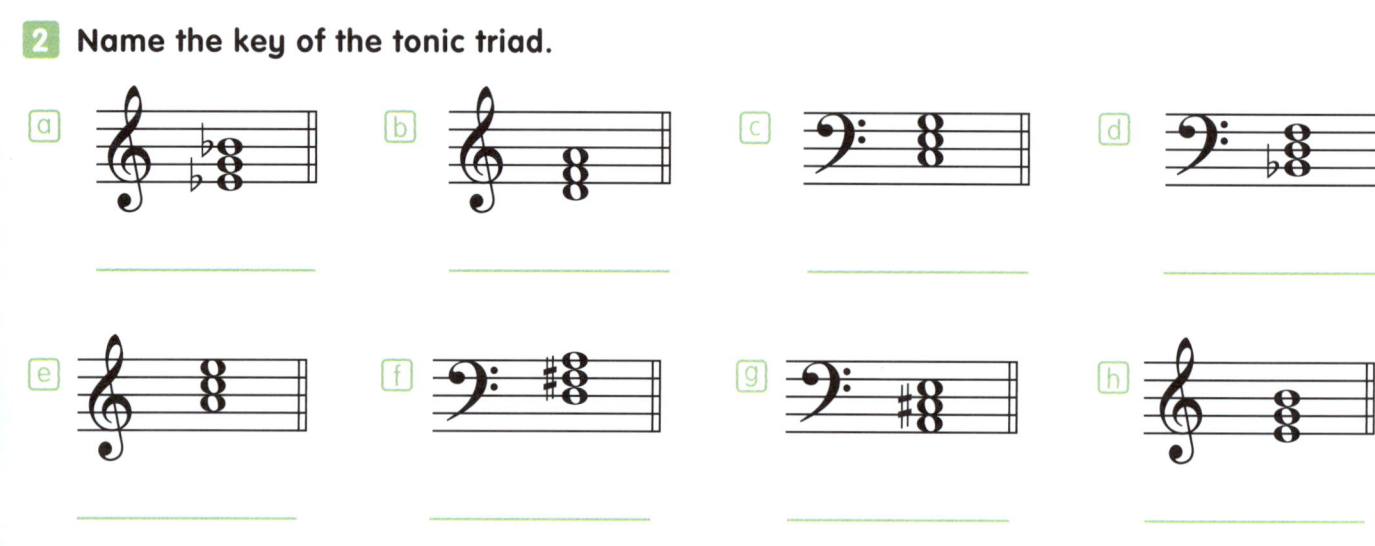

a) E G B

b) □ □ □

c) □ □ □

d) □ □ □

e) □ □ □

f) □ □ □

g) □ □ □

h) □ □ □

2 Name the key of the tonic triad.

a) b) c) d)

e) f) g) h)

3 Add the clef and key signature to the tonic triad.

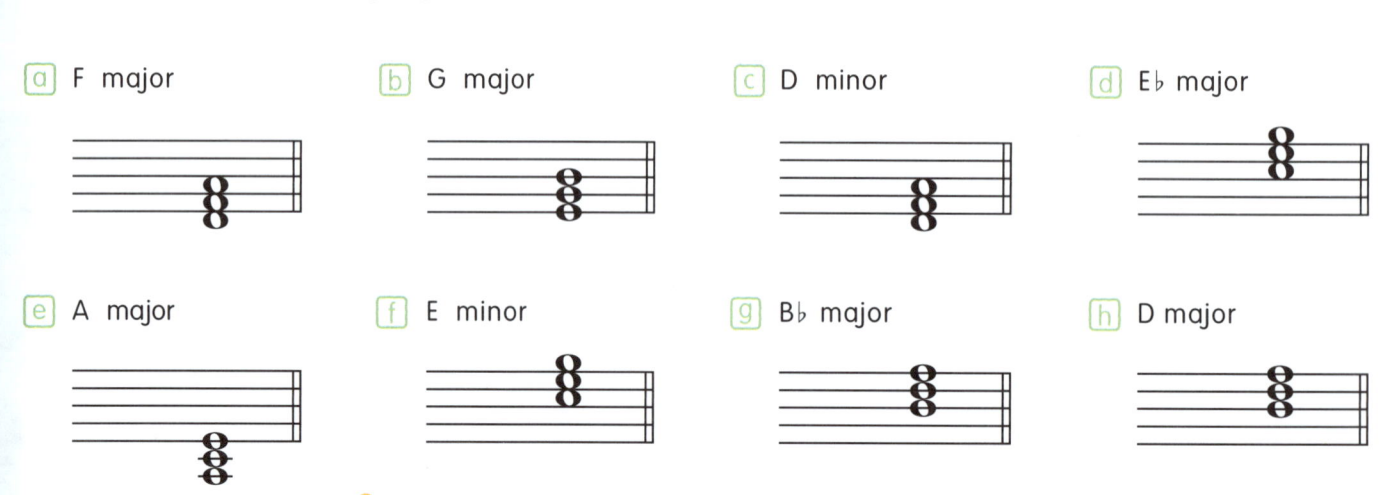

a) F major b) G major c) D minor d) E♭ major

e) A major f) E minor g) B♭ major h) D major

44 | Tonic Triads

4 Add the clef and any necessary sharps/flats to make each tonic triad. (Do not use a key signature.)

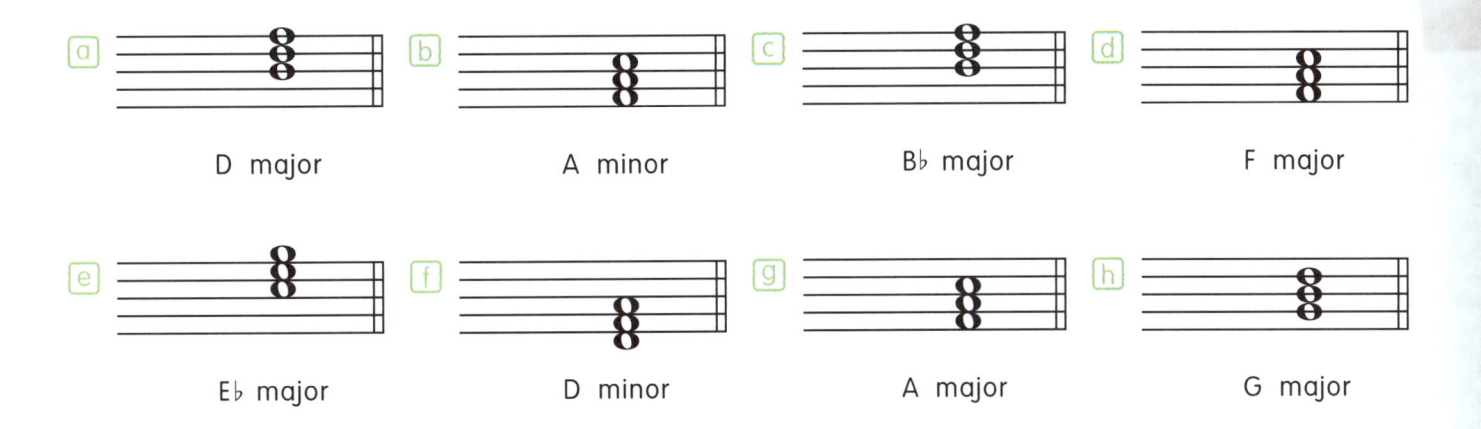

a) D major b) A minor c) B♭ major d) F major

e) E♭ major f) D minor g) A major h) G major

5 Write the tonic triad, using a key signature.

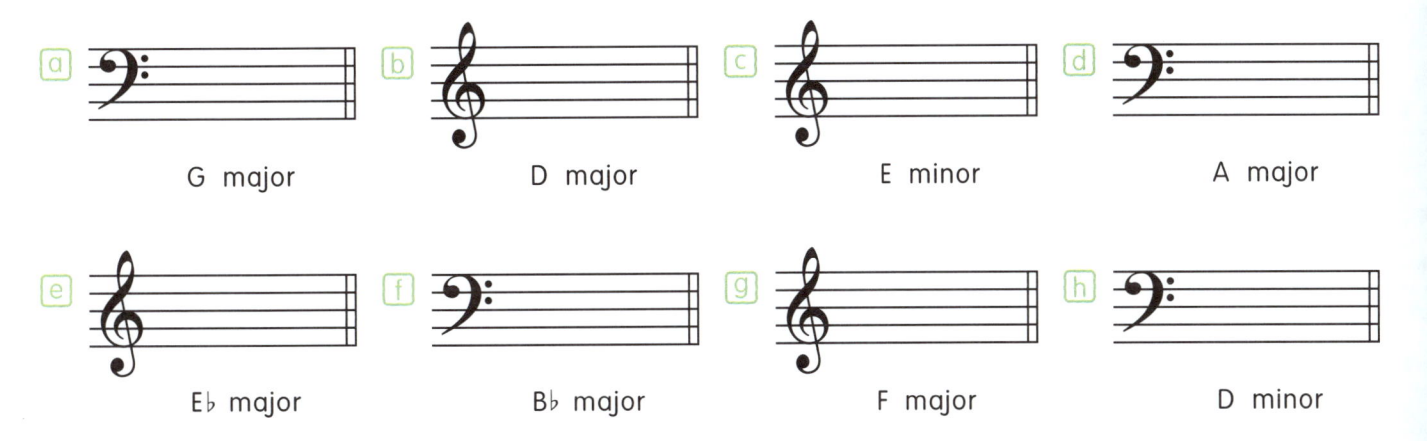

a) G major b) D major c) E minor d) A major

e) E♭ major f) B♭ major g) F major h) D minor

6 Write the tonic triad. (Do not use a key signature, but add any necessary sharps/flats.)

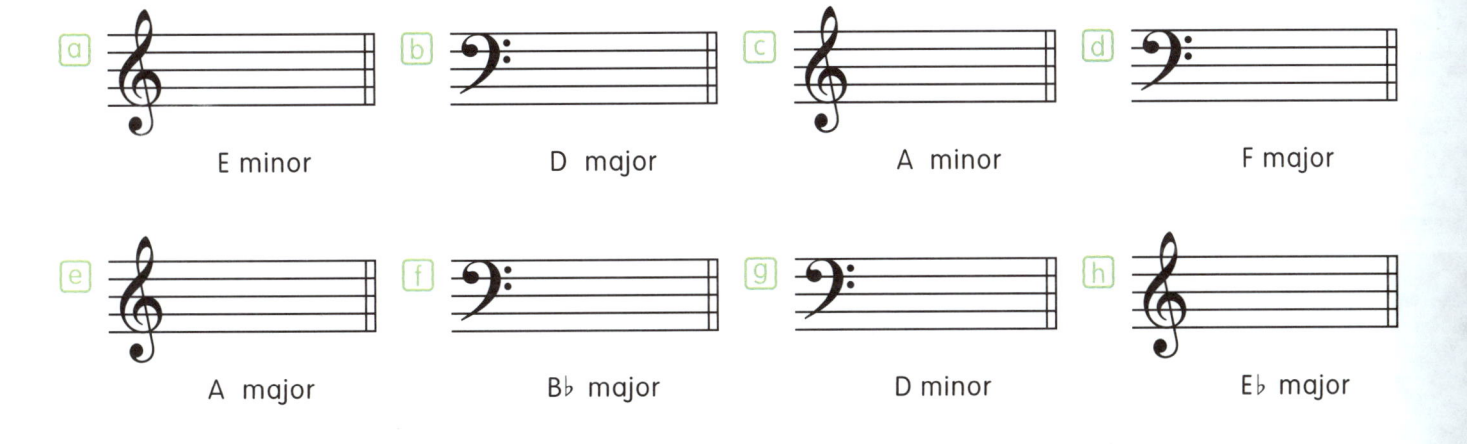

a) E minor b) D major c) A minor d) F major

e) A major f) B♭ major g) D minor h) E♭ major

Tonic Triads | 45

Degrees of the Scale

Scale degrees refer to the 7 positions of the notes.

D minor

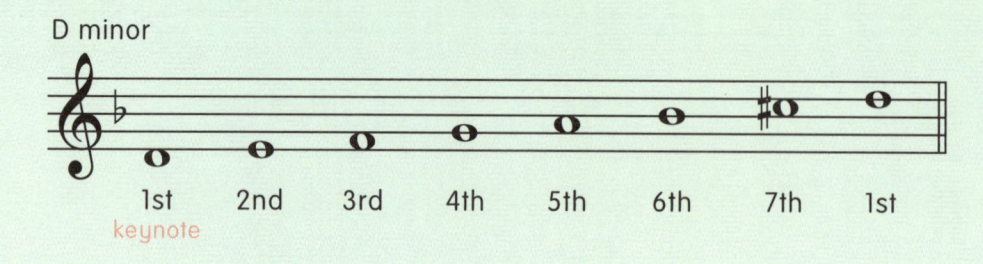

| 1st | 2nd | 3rd | 4th | 5th | 6th | 7th | 1st |

keynote

1 Write the letter name of each scale degree. Name the scale degree (1st, 2nd etc.) of each note.

a A minor

Degree	1st	2nd	3rd	4th	5th	6th	7th	1st
Letter name	A							

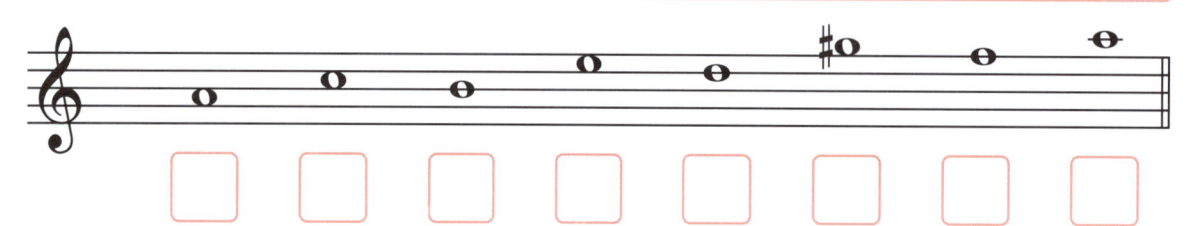

b B♭ major

Degree	1st	2nd	3rd	4th	5th	6th	7th	1st
Letter name								

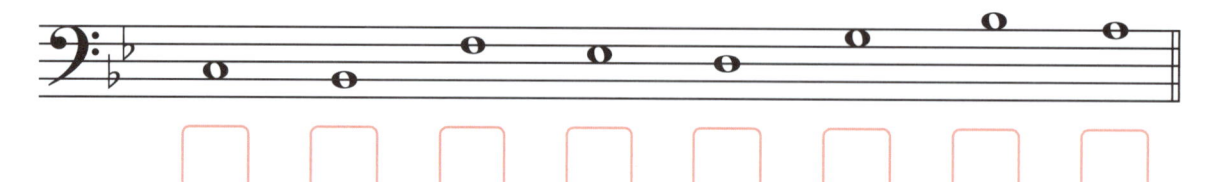

c E minor

Degree	1st	2nd	3rd	4th	5th	6th	7th	1st
Letter name								

46 | Degrees of the Scale

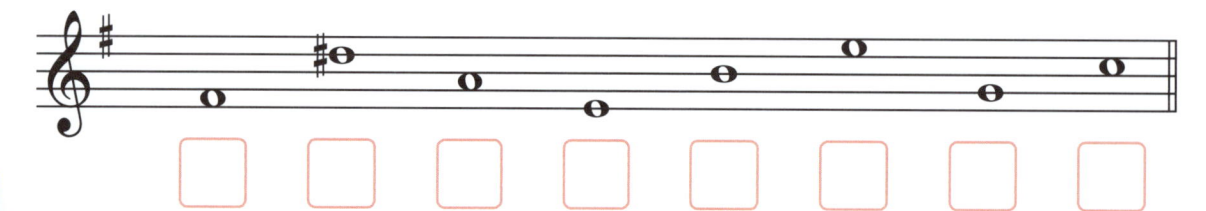

2 Name the scale degree (1st, 2nd etc.) of each note marked ∗.

a. A major

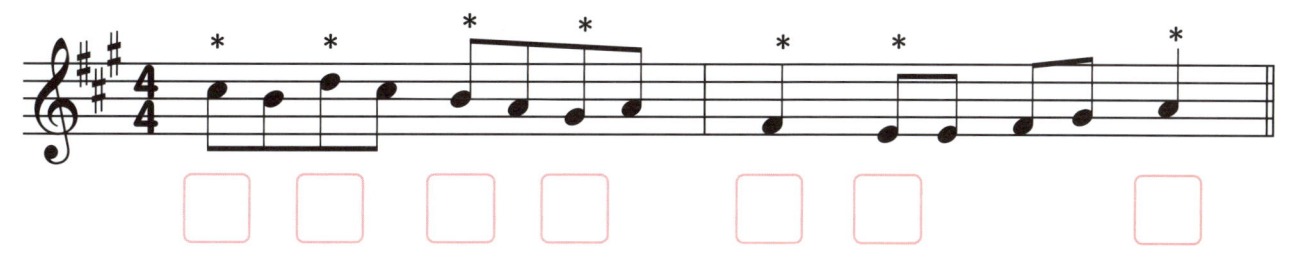

b. D minor

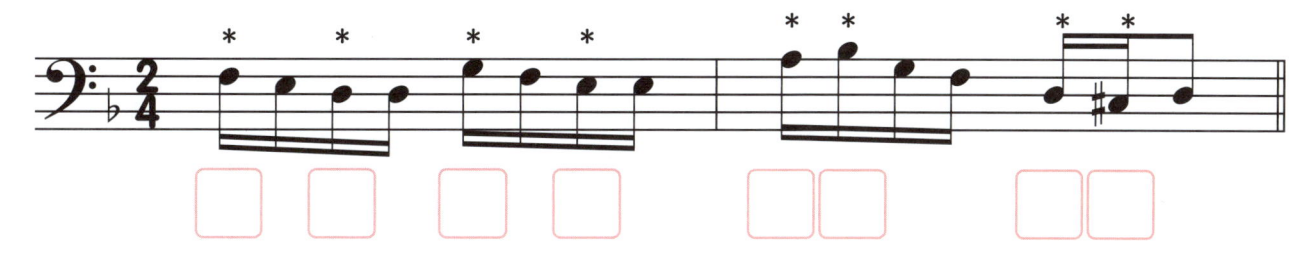

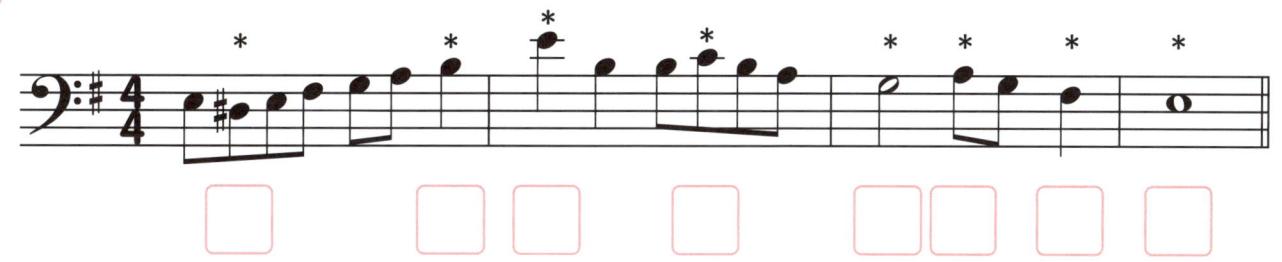

c. E minor

3 Answer the questions.

B♭ major

a. The melody begins on the _____ scale degree (1st, 2nd etc.).

b. Name the degree of the scale of the first note of bar 3. _____

c. The melody ends on the _____ scale degree (1st, 2nd etc.).

d. Circle a note that is the 7th degree of the scale.

Degrees of the Scale | 47

Intervals

An **interval** is the distance between 2 notes.

Harmonic interval

E minor — keynote — 2nd — 3rd — 4th — 5th — 6th — 7th — 8th/8ve

Melodic interval

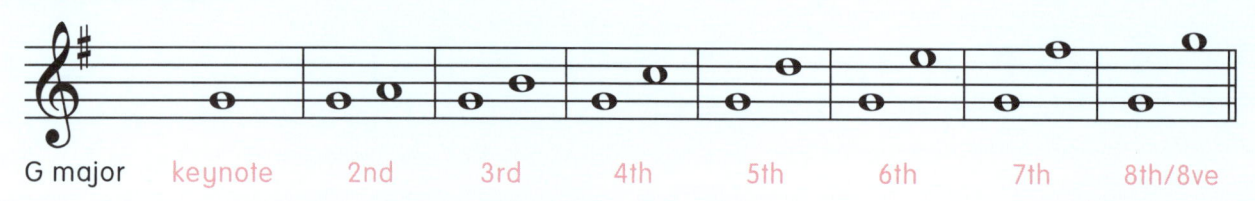

G major — keynote — 2nd — 3rd — 4th — 5th — 6th — 7th — 8th/8ve

1 Write the number (2nd, 3rd etc.) of the harmonic interval.

a) A major

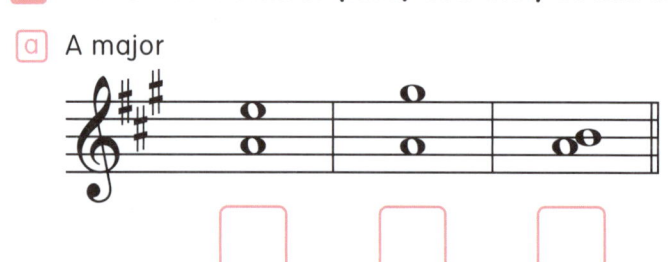

b) E minor

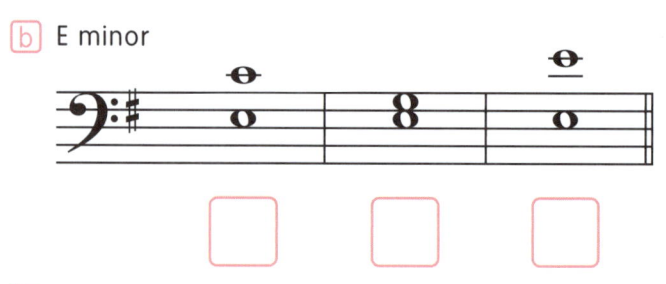

c) B♭ major

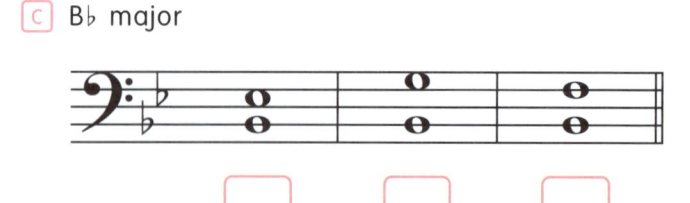

d) D minor

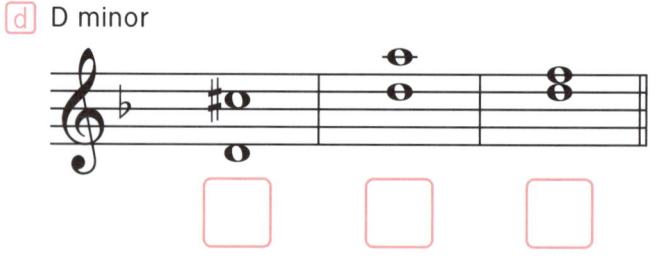

2 Write a note above each note to form the harmonic interval.

a) D major — 2nd, 8th/8ve, 5th

b) A minor — 4th, 6th, 3rd

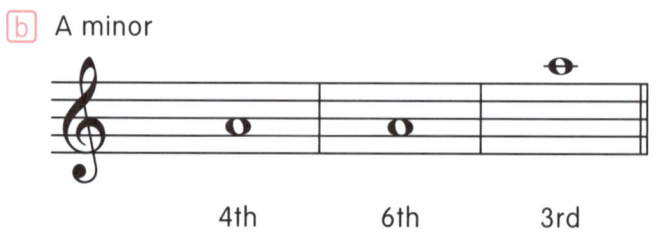

c) G major — 6th, 3rd, 8th/8ve

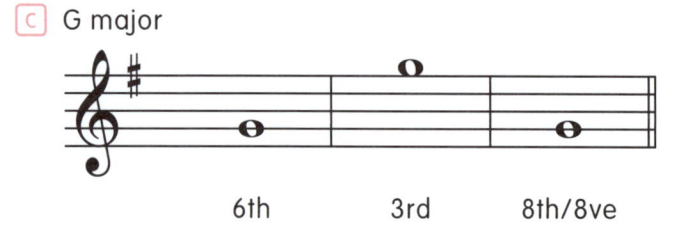

d) E♭ major — 5th, 2nd, 7th

48 | Intervals

3 Write the number (2nd, 3rd etc.) of the melodic interval.

a D major

b E minor

c B♭ major

d A major

4 Write a higher note after each note to form the melodic interval.

a G major

    5th   2nd   7th

b E♭ major

    6th   3rd   8th/8ve

c A major

    4th   6th   2nd

d D minor

    5th   8th/8ve   3rd

5 Circle 2 notes next to each other that are

a a 4th apart

b a 5th apart

c a 6th apart

d an octave (8th/8ve) apart

Intervals | 49

Composing Four-Bar Rhythms

Composing a 4-bar rhythm

Repetition and **contrast** are important in music.
- Repetition, an exact repeat of a rhythmic pattern, creates unity.
- Contrast, a new rhythmic pattern, adds variety and interest.

Using the ABAC plan
A's are entirely identical (repeated) and B and C are entirely different (contrasting).
- Bar 1: Given pattern (A).
- Bar 2: New pattern (B).
- Bar 3: Repeat of A (A).
- Bar 4: Different pattern from that of A and B, with a long note ending (C).

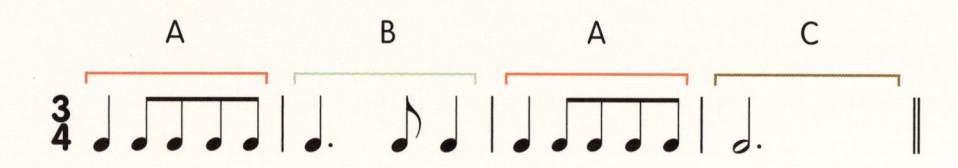

1 Colour each pattern with a different colour.

a) ABAC plan

b) ABBC plan

c) ABCB plan

d) ABCD plan

2 Use ⌐⌐ to mark any bars with the same rhythmic pattern. Write the plan of the melody.

a)

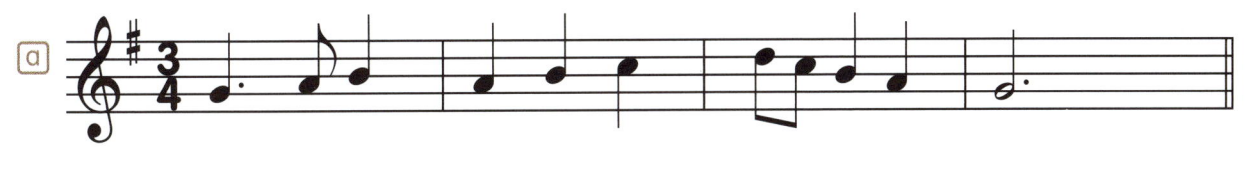

Plan: _____

b)

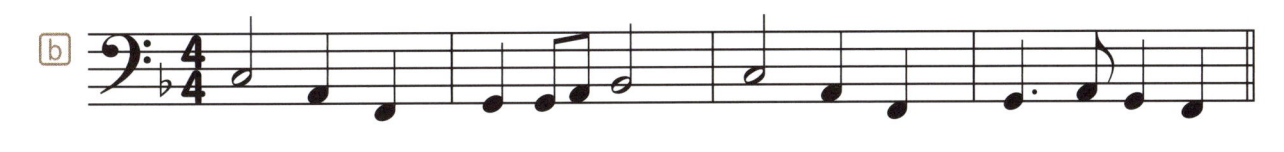

Plan: _____

c)

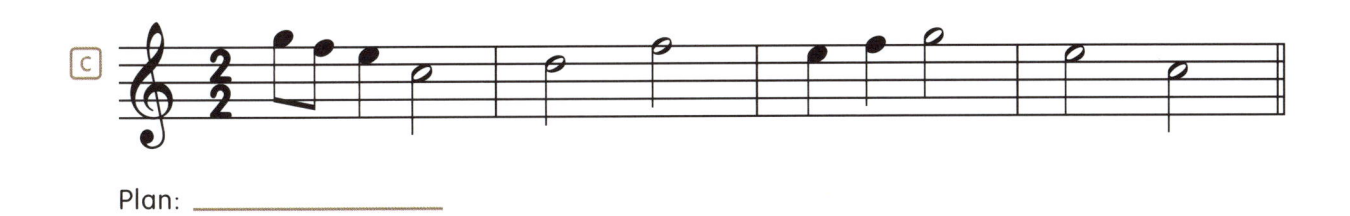

Plan: _____

d)

Plan: _____

e)

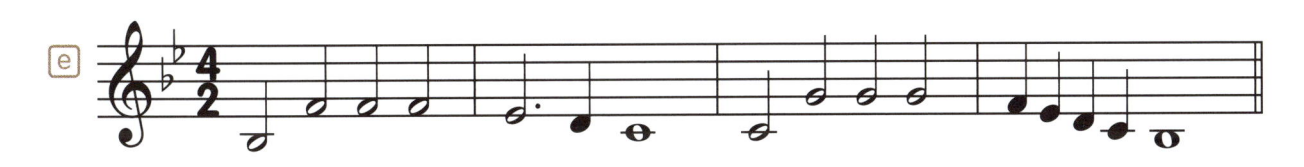

Plan: _____

f)

Plan: _____

Composing Four-Bar Rhythms | 51

3 Write a four-bar rhythm, using the ABAC plan.

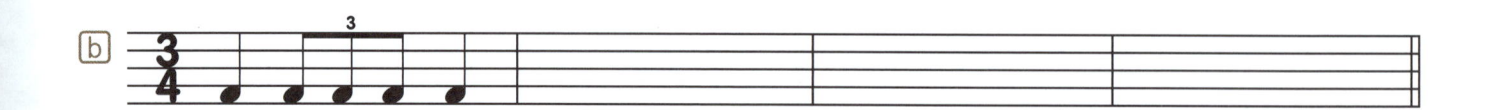

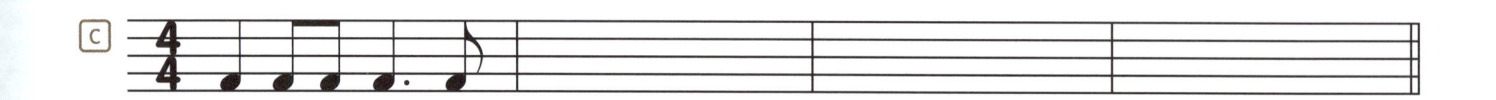

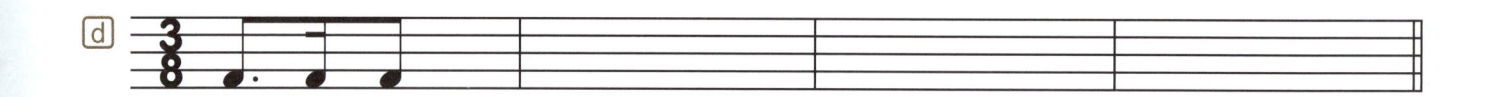

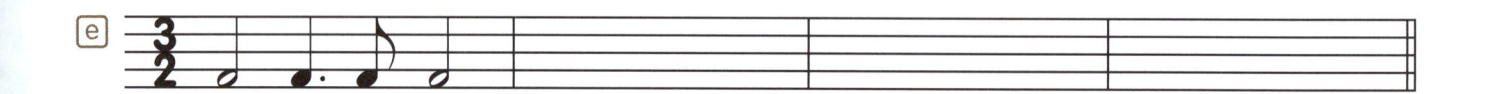

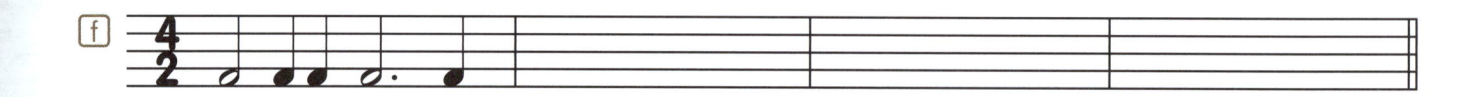

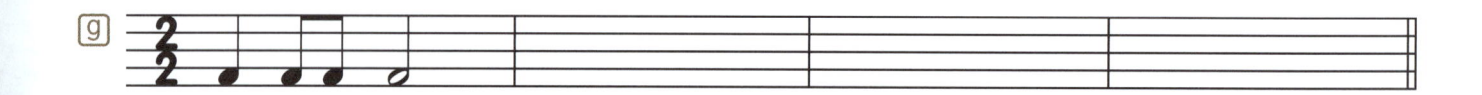

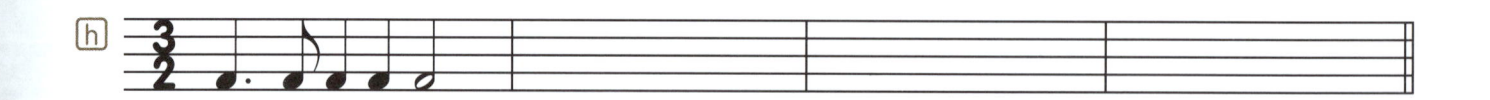

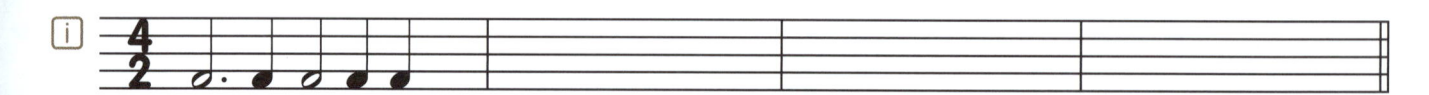

52 | Composing Four-Bar Rhythms

Performance Directions

Newly introduced terms for Grade 2 are highlighted in bold.

Tempo

accelerando (accel.)	gradually getting faster
adagio	slow
allargando	getting broader, louder and slower
allegretto	fairly fast
allegro	lively, fast
allegro assai	very fast
andante	at a walking pace
andantino	faster or slower than andante
larghetto	rather slow
largo	slow, stately
lento	slow
moderato	moderately (**allegro moderato**: moderately fast)
mosso, moto	movement (**meno mosso**: slower; **con moto**: with movement)
presto	very fast
rallentando (rall.)	gradually getting slower
ritardando (ritard., rit.)	gradually getting slower
ritenuto (riten.,rit.)	held back
tempo	speed, time (a tempo: in time)
vivace/vivo	fast, lively

Style and mood

alla marcia	in the style of a march
cantabile	in a singing style
da capo (D.C.)	repeat from the beginning
dal segno (D.S.)	repeat from the sign 𝄋
dolce	soft, sweet
espressivo (espress., espr.)	expressive
fine	the end
giocoso	merry
grave	very slow, solemn
grazioso	gracefully
legato	smoothly
maestoso	majestic
simile (sim.)	in the same way
sostenuto	sustained
staccato (stacc.)	detached
tenuto	held

Dynamics

crescendo (cresc.)	getting louder	*fz* (forzando)		forced, accented
decrescendo (decresc.)	getting softer	*mf* (mezzo forte)		moderately loud
diminuendo (dim.)	getting softer	*mp* (mezzo piano)		moderately soft
f (forte)	loud	*p* (piano)		soft
ff (fortissimo)	very loud	*pp* (pianissimo)		very soft
fp (fortepiano)	loud, then soft	*sf*, *sfz* (sforzando, sforzato)		forced, accented

Others

a	at, to, by, for, in, in the style of	mezzo	half
al, alla	in the style of	molto	very, much
assai	very	non	not
con, col	with	piu	more
e, ed	and	poco	a little
ma	but	senza	without
meno	less	troppo	too much (non troppo: not too much)

Musical Signs

Sign	Meaning	Sign	Meaning
𝄐	pause	(crescendo)	gradually getting louder
>	accent the note	(diminuendo)	gradually getting softer
^	accent the note strongly	8va	octave
•	staccato, detached	8va / 8	play an octave higher
semi-staccato	semi-staccato	8va / 8	play an octave lower
super-staccato	super-staccato	𝄆 and 𝄇	repeat marks
—	give the note a slight pressure	M.M. ♩ = 88 or ♩ = 88	88 crotchet beats in a minute
♩.	the dot makes the note longer by half its value		
tie	tie: play only the 1st note		
slur	slur: play the notes smoothly		

Performance Directions

1 **Give the meaning of each of these:**

a accelerando (accel.) _____

b adagio _____

c allargando _____

d andante _____

e allegro _____

f allegretto _____

g largo _____

h presto _____

i ritardando (ritard., rit.) _____

j ritenuto (riten., rit.) _____

k a tempo _____

l vivace, vivo _____

m alla marcia _____

n dolce _____

o cantabile _____

p espressivo (espress., espr.) _____

q giocoso _____

r grave _____

s grazioso _____

t fine _____

u legato _____

v maestoso _____

w staccato (stacc.) _____

x sostenuto _____

y sforzando (sf, sfz) _____

z tenuto _____

Performance Directions | 55

General Exercises

Answer the questions.

Moderato

a Letter names

i Write the letter name of the lowest note. _____

ii Write the letter name of the highest note. _____

iii Write the letter name of the last note in bar 3. _____

b Time names and time values

i Write the time name (e.g. crotchet, minim) of the shortest note. _____

ii Write the time name (e.g. crotchet, minim) of the longest note. _____

iii The tied notes in bars 1-2 are worth _____ quavers.

iv The last note in bar 4 is worth _____ semiquavers.

v How many bars contain a minim? _____

vi Cross out any time values that are NOT used:

| semibreve | dotted minim | minim | crotchet | quaver | semiquaver |

c Time signatures

i The bottom number **2** in $\frac{3}{2}$ means minim beats. _____ (TRUE/UNTRUE)

ii Rewrite the rhythm of bars 1-2 using the new time signature.

$\frac{3}{4}$

d Notes and rests

i The rhythm ♫ occurs _____ times.

ii Which bar has the same rhythm as bar 1? Bar _____

iii A triplet means 3 quavers are played in the time of a _____ .

56 | General Exercises

2 Answer the questions.

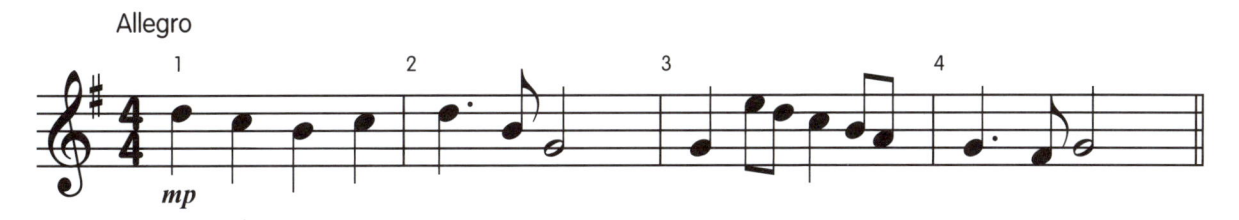

Allegro

a Tones and semitones
i Use ⌐⌐ to mark any pair of notes which make a semitone.
ii Circle any pair of notes that make a tone.

b Scales
i   Name the key of the melody. _____
ii Which other key has the same key signature? _____
iii This piece uses all the notes of the G major scale. _____ (TRUE/UNTRUE)
iv Use ⌐⌐ to mark the first 5 notes of the G major scale.

c Degrees of the scale
i The melody begins on the _____ scale degree (1st, 2nd etc.).
ii The melody ends on the _____ scale degree (1st, 2nd etc.).

d Intervals
i Write the number (2nd, 3rd etc.) of the interval between the last 2 notes of bar 2. _____
ii Circle 2 notes next to each other that are a 6th apart.

e Tonic triads
i How many bars contain all the notes of the tonic triad? _____
ii Which bar has only notes of the tonic triad? Bar _____

General Exercises | 57

3 **Answer the questions.**

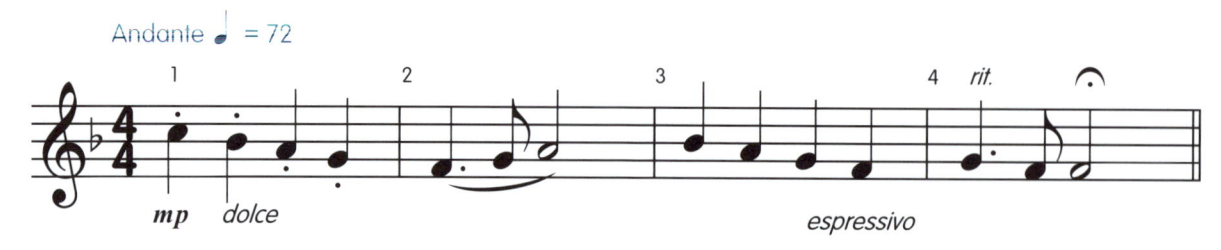

a **Performance directions**

i Copy the melody accurately. (Include the clef, key signature, time signature and all other details.)

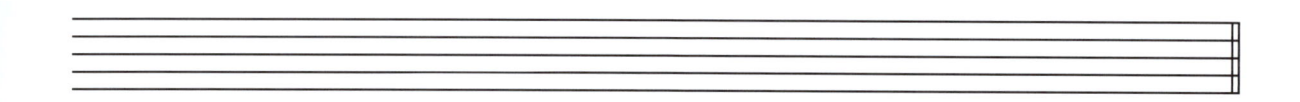

ii Give the meaning of each of these:

Andante _____

♩ = 72 _____

mp _____

dolce _____

espressivo _____

rit. _____

the dots above notes (bar 1) _____

iii All the notes are marked to be played legato (smoothly) in bar _____ .

iv All the notes are marked to be played staccato (detached) in bar _____ .

v The performer is told to pause or hold the note in bar _____ .

58 | General Exercises

Specimen Test Grade 2

TOTAL MARKS
100

Duration: 1 ½ hours

1 Add the missing bar-lines.　　10

2 Write a four-bar rhythm.　　10

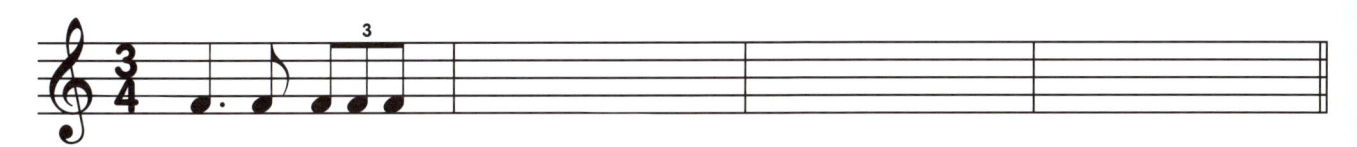

3 Write a higher note after each note to form the melodic interval named. The key is B♭ major.　　10

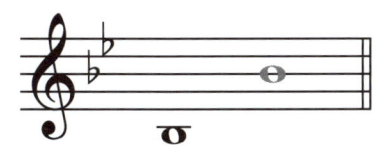

8th/8ve

3rd

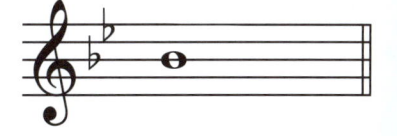

7th

4th

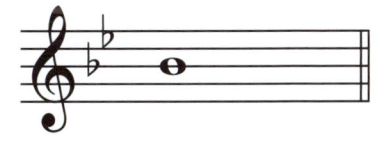

2nd

5th

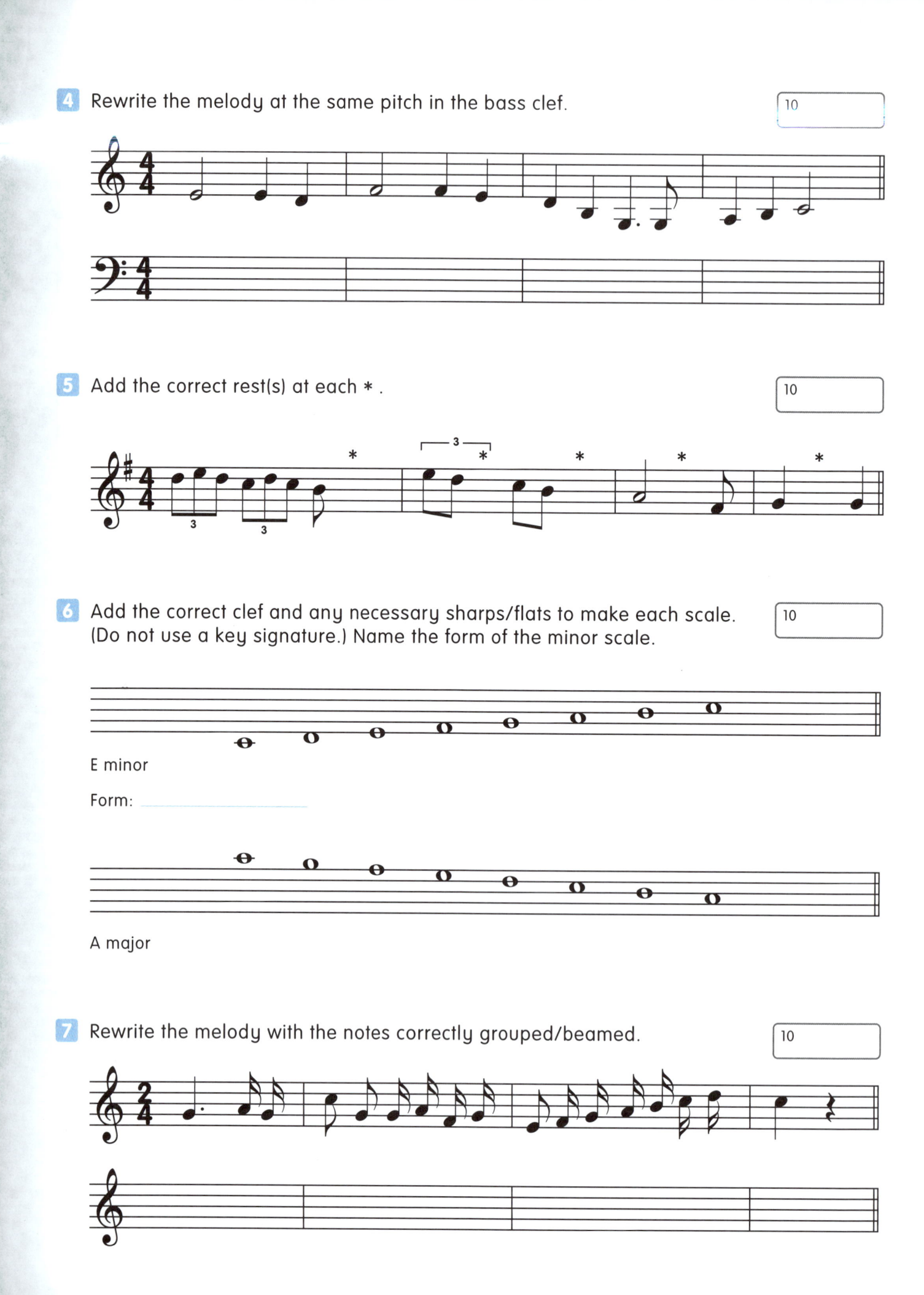

4 Rewrite the melody at the same pitch in the bass clef. [10]

5 Add the correct rest(s) at each *. [10]

6 Add the correct clef and any necessary sharps/flats to make each scale. [10]
(Do not use a key signature.) Name the form of the minor scale.

E minor

Form: _____

A major

7 Rewrite the melody with the notes correctly grouped/beamed. [10]

60 | Specimen Test Grade 2

8 Answer the questions.

(a) Copy the music from the start of bar 5 to the end of the melody accurately. [10]
(Include the clef, key signature, time signature and all other details.)

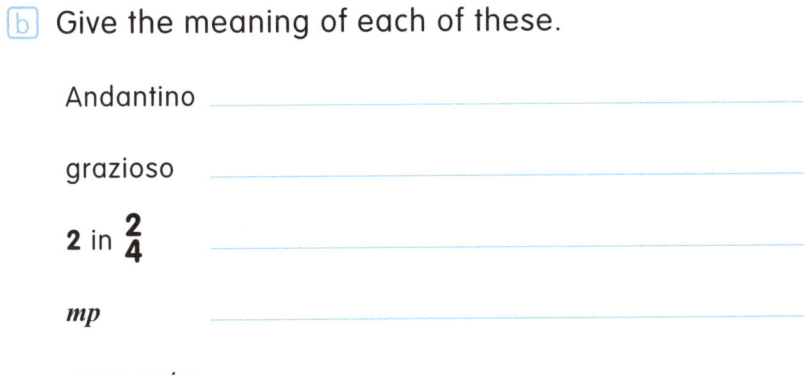

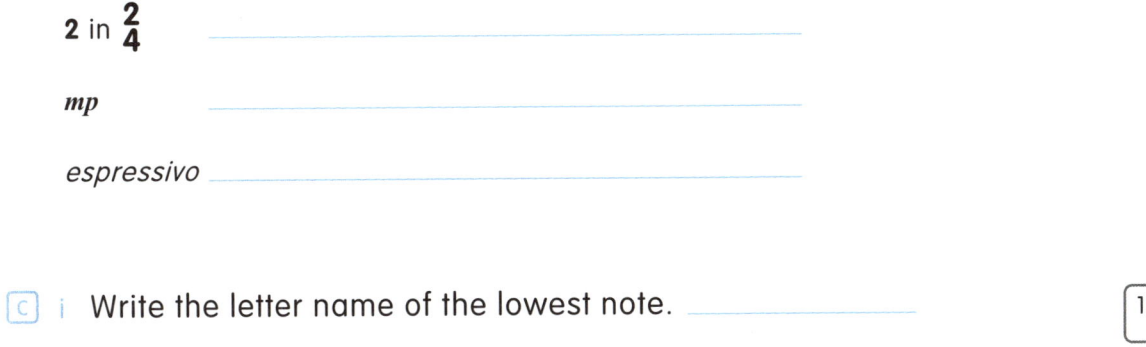

(b) Give the meaning of each of these. [10]

Andantino _____

grazioso _____

2 in 2/4 _____

mp _____

espressivo _____

(c) i Write the letter name of the lowest note. _____ [10]

ii The key is E♭ major. Which bar has all the notes of the tonic triad? Bar _____

iii Circle 2 notes next to each other that are an octave (8th/8ve) apart.

iv This rhythm ♩. ♪ occurs _____ times.

v This melody uses all the degrees of the scale (1st, 2nd etc.) of E♭ major. _____
(TRUE/FALSE)

Specimen Test Grade 2 | **61**

Revision Notes

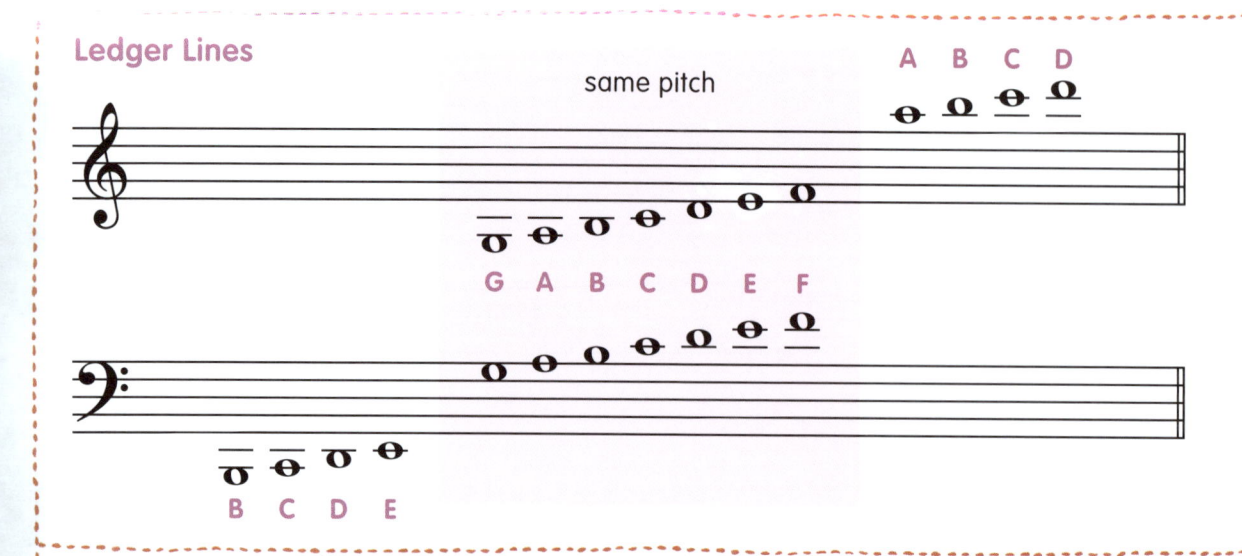

Ledger Lines

(Treble clef showing notes G A B C D E F below staff and A B C D above staff, marked "same pitch")

(Bass clef showing notes B C D E below staff and G A B C D E F above staff)

Time names and time values

Time name	Note	Rest	Time value
semibreve (whole note)	𝅝	𝄻	4
minim (half note)	𝅗𝅥	𝄼	2
crotchet (quarter note)	♩	𝄽	1
quaver (eighth note)	♪	𝄾	½
semiquaver (sixteenth note)	𝅘𝅥𝅯	𝄿	¼

Time name	Note	Time value
dotted minim (dotted half note)	𝅗𝅥.	3
dotted crotchet (dotted quarter note)	♩.	1½
dotted quaver (dotted eighth note)	♪.	¾

Whole bar rest

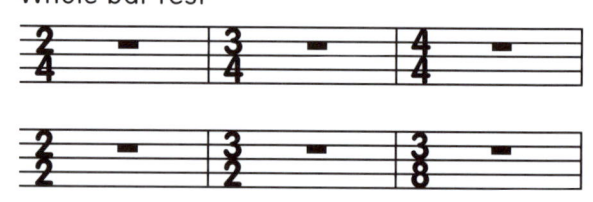

(Examples in 2/4, 3/4, 4/4, 2/2, 3/2, 3/8)

Time signatures

Simple duple	Simple triple	Simple quadruple
2/2 2 minim beats	3/2 3 minim beats	4/2 4 minim beats
2/4 2 crotchet beats	3/4 3 crotchet beats	4/4 4 crotchet beats
	3/8 3 quaver beats	

Triplets

Triplets (notes of different values)	Triplets (3 notes of the same value)	Equal to:

Key signatures of major and harmonic minor scales

	Sharp key				Flat key		
Major	C major	G major	D major	A major	F major	B♭ major	E♭ major
Key signature							
Harmonic minor	A minor (+ G♯)	E minor (+ D♯)			D minor (+ C♯)		

Grouping of notes

Minim beats

Crotchet beats

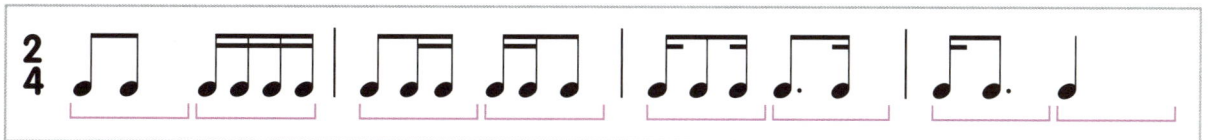

Quaver beats

Grouping of Rests

- Use a rest for every beat.

Minim beats	Crotchet beats	Quaver beats
2/2	2/4	
3/2	3/4	3/8
4/2	4/4	

Exception: In a bar of 4 beats, use a 2-beat rest for the first 2 beats/the last 2 beats.

- When a silence is less than a beat, use a rest for every subdivision of the beat.

Minim beats	Crotchet beats	Quaver beats
2/2	2/4	3/8
2/2	2/4	3/8
2/2	2/4	3/8
2/2	2/4	3/8

- When a silence is more than a beat, use as few rests as possible.

Minim beats	Crotchet beats
3/2	3/4
3/2	3/4
4/2	4/4
4/2	4/4

64 | Revision Notes